The Road to Debt Bondage

How Banks Create Unpayable Debt

Derryl Hermanutz

The Road To Debt Bondage
How Banks Create Unpayable Debt

Copyright 2018 by Derryl Hermanutz

ISBN-13: 978-1725895249

ISBN-10: 1725895242

Table Of Contents

Failure of the Credit-Debt System ... 5
   rediscovery of the money problem ... 5
   commercial banks create the money supply ... 7
   banking system failure and monetary system reform ... 9
   3 different kinds of money ... 10
   2 different money supplies ... 11
   bank account money: debiting and crediting ... 12
   "savings-funded" shadow banks ... 14
   credit-debt money ... 15
   creating (and un-creating) bank deposits ... 16
   commercial banking is a debt-based money supply creation system ... 18
   the payments system: bank deposits and bank reserves ... 20
   liquidity failure ... 23
   where is all the money? ... 24
   creditors' uncollectable credits owed as debtors' unpayable debts ... 26
   obfuscating complexification ... 30
   asset-secured credit-debt creation ... 32
   asset price inflation-deflation ... 33
   credit-fueled prosperity... ... 35
   ...turns to debt-deflation bust ... 37
   bankruptcy ... 38
   extraordinary measures ... 42
   debt-for-equity ... 44
   money liabilities (account balances) and money (currency) ... 48
   "risk-free" government debt and base money creation ... 49
   ever-increasing total debt ... 52
   governments issue debts, not money ... 54
   credit-debt expansion then Collapse ... 54
   the commercial banking system should be fixed, not replaced ... 56
   popular misconceptions ... 57
   monetary system reform ... 58

Money is Created, Not Produced ... 61
   everybody needs money ... 61
   we do not produce or create our own money ... 62
   2 different economies ... 63
   the money system is the economy's financial nervous system ... 64

Money is Numbers ... 68
   money is numbers ... 68
   monetary macroeconomics ... 72

    financial government 73
    the debt-free money solution 78

The Debt-Free Money Income **81**
    a money-funded debt reduction program 81
    zero interest perpetual bonds 82
    creating debt-free bank account money (bank deposits) within the present central-commercial banking system 83
    QE for the economy 85
    how much should the Money Income be? 86
    where would the new money go? 89
    savings and securitization 94
    how fast would debts be paid down? 96
    would the Money Income cause price inflation? 99
    the Money Income program does not replace existing monetary and fiscal programs 105
    working out the details 107
    knowing it must be done, and actually doing it 109
    different details for different countries 110
    a simple solution to a fixable problem 112

Epilogue **114**

Bibliography **116**

Failure of the Credit-Debt System

rediscovery of the money problem

Since the 2008 banking system failure, eyes and minds are re-opening to the reality that there is something deeply *wrong* with the money system itself.

But money, money creation, banking and credit-debt creation -- and the monetary-financial system within which it all works -- is a very different kind of creature than most people *think* it is.

Most people believe the government or the central bank issues the national money supply; and are not aware that virtually all of our spendable-earnable and saveable, investible payments media (money) is created by commercial banks as repayable loans of commercial bank-issued credit-debt money -- bank deposits.

Our deposit account *credit* balances are our banks' deposit liability *debt* balances.

We use commercial banks' deposit liability *debts* as our deposit account 'money' supply.

The government-printed, central bank-issued cash money supply (currency; legal tender money) we have in our pockets and cash registers and safes, is less than 5% of our total money supply.

The commercial bank-issued deposit account money supply (bank deposits; credit-debt money) we have in our commercial bank deposit accounts (and in our shadow bank cash accounts) is more than 95% of our total money supply.

We do not to any significant extent have a government-issued or central bank-issued money supply system.

We have a commercial bank-issued credit-debt creation system.

And the commercial banks' creditor-assets/debtor-liabilities "balance sheet" money supply creation system is in the midst of another one of its historic balance sheet meltdowns: a financial crisis of creditors' uncollectable money assets (credit balances) that are owed as debtors' unpayable money liabilities (debt balances).

Financial crisis is historically resolved by writing off our bank deposit account balances to relieve the commercial banking system of its unpayable deposit liability debts.

Which is what bankruptcy Trustees did in the 1930s.

And which the Dodd-Frank debt-for-equity swaps program (depositor bail-ins) plans to do this time.

Which plunges the spending-driven producer-consumer economy into Debt-Deflation Depression by writing off ruinous amounts of banks' unpayable deposit liability debts -- which used to be our spendable deposit account *money supply*.

Monetary system reformers since the 1930s have advocated government issuance of debt-free (non-repayable) money as a solution to the built-in failings of the commercial banks' debt-based "repayable bank loan and bond purchase" deposit account money supply creation system.

But largely due to widely and deeply held popular misconceptions about money, banking and credit-debt creation (which is misconceived as a government-issued money system in which commercial banks act as financial intermediaries who get loanable funds from their depositors, then lend out their depositors' savings);

and popular misconceptions about the macroeconomic workings of the world's spending-driven buy-sell for money producer-consumer economy (which is misconceived as a production-driven barter "exchange" economy in which the productive economy produces its own exchange media -- its own 'money' -- by producing stuff that has tradeable exchange value);

none of these monetarily necessary, financially and economically beneficial reform proposals have ever been implemented.

The commercial banks' near-absolute monopoly of money supply issuance remains blissfully *un*-reformed; and teetering toward its next Collapse.

So let's start by seeing how the monetary system -- the money supply creation system -- actually works.

Seeing how the banks' credit-debt creation system works, exposes why it fails, and illuminates the technically simple way to fix it: add government-issued debt-free money into the commercial bank-issued credit-debt money supply.

Though the monetary system itself is fairly simple and easy to understand, some of the realities of the system -- e.g. money is numbers with a $ sign in front of them; commercial banks create the spendable money supply by typing numbers into bank accounts; we use commercial banks' deposit liability debts as our deposit account money supply -- can be mind-repellingly hard to *believe*.

And the terminology that describes the monetary system processes is incomprehensible. But to see how the system works, we have to know what the terminology means. In this book I will attempt to translate the terminology into comprehensible language.

Once you get past the terminology the workings (and failings) of the banks' credit-debt creation system become clearly visible.

So I'll begin with a series of quotes that tell some of the story. Then I'll describe all of the basic monetary system processes in plain language that shows what the terminology actually means.

commercial banks create the money supply

"This article explains how the majority of money in the modern economy is created by commercial banks making loans. Money creation in practice differs from some popular misconceptions -- banks do not simply act as intermediaries, lending out deposits that savers place with them, and nor do they 'multiply up' central bank money to create new loans and deposits." {Bank of England, *Money Creation in the Modern Economy* (2014) pdf online}

"The purpose of this booklet is to describe the basic process of money creation in a "fractional reserve" banking system. The approach taken illustrates the changes in bank balance sheets that occur when deposits in banks change as a result of monetary actions by the Federal Reserve System -- the central bank of the United States.

...*What is money?* If money is viewed simply as a tool used to facilitate transactions, only those media that are readily accepted in exchange for goods, services and other assets need to be considered (as) transactions money." {Federal Reserve Bank of Chicago, *Modern Money Mechanics: A Workbook on Bank Reserves and Deposit Expansion* (first published 1961, last updated 1994); pdf online}

"...the liabilities of banks and other depository institutions have the peculiar characteristic *that they are money*. When these intermediaries purchase earning assets such as bank loans and promissory notes, they pay for them by issuing their own liabilities. There is no question of the public's accepting the liabilities of depository institutions... The public accepts them because they are accepted as money by others.

Thus, by increasing their earning assets, these institutions at the same time add to the supply of money. The creation of deposits by depository institutions to make loans or acquire securities represents in each case the creation of new deposits. We are now in a position to express our *first fundamental principle of deposit creation* by depository institutions.

Through the creation of a deposit by making a loan or acquiring a security, a depository institution increases the money supply by the amount of the created deposit." {Shearer, Chant, Bond, *Economics of the Canadian Financial System: Theory, Policy & Institutions* Third Edition (1995); from a section titled, Banks and Deposit Creation, p. 565; italics in original}

"This means that banks can create book money just by making an accounting entry: according to the Bundesbank's economists, this refutes a popular misconception that banks act simply as intermediaries at the time of lending -- i.e. that banks can only grant credit using funds placed with them previously as deposits by other customers. By the same token, excess central bank reserves are not a necessary precondition for a bank to grant credit (and thus create money)." {Deutsche Bundesbank Eurosystem, *How money is created* (from the English language summary published April 25, 2017 on the Bundesbank's website); pdf online}

"There are three main types of money: currency, bank deposits, and central bank reserves. ...Most money in the modern economy is in the form of bank deposits, which are created by commercial banks themselves."
{Bank of England, *Money in the Modern Economy* (2014); pdf online}

banking system failure and monetary system reform

"The most outstanding fact of the last depression is the destruction of 8 billion dollars -- over a third -- of our "check-book money" -- demand deposits." {Irving Fisher, *100% Money and the Public Debt* (1936)}

"In *Booms and Depressions* (1932), I have developed, theoretically and statistically, what may be called a debt-deflation theory of great depressions..." {Irving Fisher, *The Debt-Deflation Theory of Great Depressions* (1933)}

"The Proposal: 1. A reform of the monetary and banking system to eliminate both the private creation or destruction of money... The private creation of money can perhaps best be eliminated by adopting the 100 per cent reserve proposal, thereby separating the depository from the lending function of the banking system.

...These modifications would leave as the chief monetary functions of the banking system the provision of depository facilities, the facilitation of check clearance, and the like; and as the chief function of the monetary authorities, the creation of money to meet government deficits or the retirement of money when the government has a surplus." {Milton Friedman, *A Monetary and Fiscal Framework for Economic Stability* (1948) pdf online}

"In short: Nationalize money but do not nationalize banking. In fact the present demand to nationalize banking would fade away if only the control of money were recaptured by Government. Moreover, in my opinion, almost all of our complicated and vexatious banking laws could be repealed if once we made this separation between money creation and money lending. The insurance of bank deposits would become unnecessary, because there would be no reason for runs on banks.

...We have noted several advantages of the 100% plan...the unification of our two sorts of money by making deposit money into genuine money in trust so that the average man can understand the money system." {Irving Fisher, *100% Money and the Public Debt* (1936)}

"Over the past thirty years, we have been moving from a bank credit system to a capital markets credit system... Under the old "legacy" banking system, banks made loans and funded those loans with deposit liabilities.

...In the new "shadow banking" system, by contrast, loans were transformed into securities, and investors in those securities funded their positions in the wholesale money market using asset-backed commercial paper, repurchase agreements, or simply unsecured short term borrowing (Eurodollars)...but *the ultimate liquidity backstop proved to be lines of credit with the legacy banking system.* Solvency risk was handled by credit enhancements using interest rate swaps and credit default swaps, so *the ultimate solvency backstop was the capital buffer on the balance sheet of swap counterparties.*

...The credit crisis that began in August 2007 involved failure of both the liquidity and the solvency risk systems... Today we see more clearly that the new system was not so much an independent alternative to the existing system as it was symbiotic with it, intertwined at multiple levels including the level of regulatory support through the Fed and FDIC." {Perry Mehrling, *The Global Credit Crisis, and Policy Response* (2009); pdf online; my italics}

3 different kinds of money

Money is created by the monetary system: the central-commercial banking system.

There are 3 different kinds of money: currency (legal tender money); bank deposits (credit-debt money); central bank reserves (base money); that are created by 3 different monetary system processes.

Central bank reserves -- commercial banks' reserve account balances in their central bank reserve accounts -- are banking system money (base money) that banks pay each other; not part of the economy's spendable-earnable money supply.

We use currency (the spendable banknotes and coins in our pockets); and bank deposits (the spendable balances in our commercial bank deposit accounts; and the investible balances in our shadow bank cash accounts); as our money supply.

The central bank issues the base money supply -- reserve account balances and vault cash -- to commercial banks.

Commercial banks issue the spendable money supply -- deposit account balances and cash withdrawals -- to the money-using economy: people, businesses, governments.

Insofar as commercial banks are "financial intermediaries": they intermediate between the base money supply-issuing central bank; and the spendable money supply-using economy.

Commercial banks do not get loanable funds from their depositors then lend out and invest their customers' account balances.

That's what *shadow banks* do, in the savings-funded capital markets financial system: the "shadow banking" system. Brokerages, investment banks, etc are "shadow banks".

Commercial banks are monetary system institutions -- depository institutions: deposit-*creating* institutions.

Commercial banks *create* the bank deposits that they lend.

Commercial banks create the spendable money supply in the form of the deposit account money supply: by making repayable loans of newly-created bank deposits to private sector loan account debtors and to government bond debtors.

2 different money supplies

The government doesn't print cash money and spend it into the economy.

Currency is sold into the economy via the central and commercial banks.

In countries (like the US) where the government owns the Printer and Mint: the central bank buys banknotes from the Printer and coins from the Mint and pays for its currency purchases by typing spendable credits into the government's central bank account balance. {This is the only spendable money the central bank creates for the government: when the central bank monetizes the currency.}

Commercial banks buy currency from the central bank and pay with debits to their central bank reserve account balances.

Then we create the spendable cash money supply when we make cash withdrawals and pay with debits to our commercial bank deposit account balances.

We have 2 different money supplies -- the cash money supply in our pockets; and the deposit account money supply in our bank accounts -- that are made of 2 different kinds of money: currency and bank deposits.

Currency is physical money, pocket money: paperlike banknotes and metal coins. We pay each other currency in direct hand to hand payments of banknotes and coins from buyers of stuff to sellers of the stuff; from money-spenders to money-earners; from money-investors to money-earners; from money-*payers* to money-*payees*.

Bank deposits are digital money, bank account money: electronic digits in banking system accounting software. We pay each other bank deposits -- by check, direct deposit, online banking, debit card, smartphone payment, etc -- within the central-commercial bank-operated payments system of debiting (subtracting) the payments out of payers' bank deposit account balances and crediting (adding) the payments into payees' bank deposit account balances.

bank account money: debiting and crediting

Look at your bank deposit account statement. The Debits column is you paying bank deposits out of your payer bank deposit account into payees' bank deposit accounts. The Credits column is other payers paying bank deposits into your payee bank deposit account. Your bank deposit account is both a payer account and a payee account. The number at the bottom of the Running Balance column -- your deposit account *balance* -- is the money. "Bank deposits".

The number -- your deposit account *balance* -- doesn't represent some more "real" form of money that exists somewhere else. The number *is the money*.

Nothing physically moves within the payments system. No cash money or gold or "economic value" is moved from bank account to bank account or transported from bank to bank.

The payments are subtracted (debited) out of payers' bank deposit account balances and added (credited) to payees' bank deposit account balances.

Most of the debiting and crediting is performed electronically by banking system accounting software; not by bank workers typing on keyboards.

We do not have direct access to our bank account money. When we pay a utility bill by online banking; or pay a merchant with our debit card: we authorize our bank to debit the payment amount out of our payer bank deposit account balance; and at the same time we authorize the payee's bank to credit the payment amount into the payee's bank deposit account balance.

Banks do the actual debiting and crediting of their customers' bank account balances.

The central bank debits and credits commercial banks' reserve account balances.

Commercial banks debit and credit their customers' deposit account balances.

The government has bank accounts in commercial banks and in the central bank. Commercial banks debit and credit the government's commercial bank deposit account balances. The central bank debits and credits the government's central bank account balance.

Shadow banks -- brokerages, investment banks, etc -- debit and credit their customers' cash account balances.

The bank account money -- the deposit account balances, reserve account balances, and cash account balances -- are paid out by banks debiting (subtracting from) payer account balances; and paid in by banks crediting (adding to) payee account balances.

The only money we have direct access to is the cash money supply in our pockets, which is less than 5% of our total money supply.

95-97% of all money is the deposit account money supply: the spendable, investible (and saveable) deposit account balances in our commercial bank deposit accounts; and the investible cash account balances in our shadow bank cash accounts.

"savings-funded" shadow banks

To "fund" -- to put money in -- your brokerage account (or other shadow bank account): you transfer a balance out of your commercial bank deposit account, into your shadow bank cash account. Your commercial bank debits the transfer amount out of your commercial bank deposit account balance; and your brokerage credits the transfer amount into your brokerage cash account balance.

Then you spend (invest) your cash balance buying income-generating financial assets like stocks (dividend-paying equity-assets); bonds (interest-paying debt-assets); and money market funds (loaned-out cash balances, which are interest-paying debt-assets).

When we buy assets: our brokerage debits the payment amount out of our payer cash account balance; and the asset-seller's brokerage credits the payment amount into the asset-seller's payee cash account balance.

[Our invested money is not "in" the investment. The money -- the cash balance -- is now in the asset-seller's cash account. The income-generating equity-assets and debt-assets are now in our brokerage account. The asset-seller now owns the money. We now own the assets. We *spent* our cash balance when we *bought* the investment assets. To convert our assets into spendable, investible money, we have to sell the assets to somebody who will pay their money to buy our assets. During financial crises -- which are monetary-banking system failures that destroy bank deposits -- it may not be possible to sell your assets for money, except at steeply discounted (deflated) prices: like stocks after 1929; and stocks and real estate after 2008.]

Shadow banks debit and credit their customers' cash account balances; in the same way commercial banks debit and credit their customers' deposit account balances; in the same way central banks debit and credit commercial banks' reserve account balances.

There is no cash money (currency) "in" our shadow bank cash accounts; just like there is no cash money "on deposit" in our commercial bank deposit accounts. We have commercial bank-issued bank deposits in our commercial bank deposit accounts and in our shadow bank cash accounts.

The "savings-funded" capital markets financial system is *funded* with bank deposits that are created by the commercial banking system; then transferred into shadow bank cash accounts.

credit-debt money

Bank deposits -- spendable, cashable balances in commercial bank deposit accounts -- are not originally created by people depositing cash money in banks.

We do not have cash money "on deposit" in our banks' vaults.

We have bank deposits in our bank deposit accounts.

Bank deposits are *credit-debt* instruments that commercial banks create to "fund" their bank loans to private sector debtors; and to fund their bond purchases from government debtors.

Our deposit account *credit* balances are our banks' deposit liability *debt* balances.

We have commercial banks' deposit liability *debts* in our bank deposit accounts.

creating (and un-creating) bank deposits

Commercial banks create new bank deposits in debtors' bank deposit accounts: when banks make loans with private sector debtors; and when banks purchase securities (interest-bearing Treasury bills, notes bonds: government bond debts) from government debtors.

To fund its bank loan or bond purchase, the bank types a number -- a bank deposit -- into the Credits column of the debtor's bank deposit account. The credit adds to the debtor's spendable bank deposit account *balance*.

Making a bank loan or bond purchase creates a linked pair of credits/debts: a new spendable, cashable credit balance (a new bank deposit: e.g. +$1000) in the debtor's bank deposit account; and an equal new interest-bearing, repayable debt balance (-$1000) in the debtor's bank loan or bond account.

Debtors spend their new bank loans and bond sale proceeds.

Debtors pay the new bank deposits to payees, within the bank-operated payments system.

The new credit balances are debited out of the debtors' bank deposit account balances and credited into the first payees' bank deposit account balances.

That's where the deposit account money supply -- the spendable, investible, saveable (and cashable) credit balances in our bank deposit accounts -- comes from, in the first place.

Then payees create the cash money supply by making cash withdrawals, and paying with debits to our deposit account credit balances.

But most bank deposits are never cashed-out.

Most money never exists in any other form than credit balances -- bank deposits: the deposit account money supply -- in payees' bank deposit accounts.

Debtors owe the deposit account money supply back to their creditor-banks, as payment of the debtors' unpaid -- but still owing -- loan account debt balances and bond debts.

Repaying a bank loan, or redeeming a bank-held bond, un-creates -- extinguishes; cancels out to $0/$0 -- the deposit account credit balance (+$1000) and the loan account or bond debt balance (-$1000) that were created by making the bank loan or bond purchase.

But debtors can't pay back and extinguish the deposit account credit balances because debtors don't *have* the bank deposits. All of the bank deposits are in *payees'* bank deposit accounts.

Commercial banks do not create money (currency) or lend money and debtors do not pay back money.

Debtors and their creditor-banks create credit-debt: bank deposits.

Paying the loan account debt balances with the deposit account credit balances uncreates the credit-debt money; cancels out the bank deposits, and cancels out the loan account and bond debts.

The deposit account money supply only *exists* so long as debtors' loan account and bond debts remain *unpaid*.

And conversely, so long as payees *keep* the bank deposits as our commercial bank savings account balances (savings) and shadow bank cash account balances (investible capital) -- rather than re-spending or re-investing the bank deposits back into the producer-consumer economy's spend-earn money stream -- debtors can't earn them back.

So debtors can't pay their debts.

commercial banking is a debt-based money supply creation system

Debtors' loan principal payments (and bond redemption payments) are *extinguished*: the paid-back bank deposit account balances are debited out of existence to extinguish (paydown) the debtors' loan account and bond debt balances. Banks earn debtors' loan and bond interest payments (and loan origination fees and other fees) as the banks' business income.

Debtors' unpaid interest-bearing loan account and bond *debt balances* are banks' *interest-earning assets*.

Commercial banks issue deposit liabilities (bank deposits: new spendable, cashable credit balances, in debtors' bank deposit accounts) to "pay for" the banks' purchases of interest-earning assets (the debtor's new interest-bearing loan account debt balance or bond debt).

Government debtors issue interest-bearing Treasury bills, notes, bonds -- "securities" -- government bond debts.

Private sector debtors issue interest-bearing loan account debts: mortgage loan debts, home equity loan debts, student loan debts, car loan debts, credit card debts, line of credit and overdraft debts, small business loan debts, corporate loan debts, institutional loan debts, etc, etc.

And commercial banks issue their own debts -- deposit liability debts: bank deposits -- to pay for the banks' purchases of those interest-earning debt-assets.

Debtors and their creditor-banks create the deposit account money supply -- and the loan account debts and bond debts owed to commercial banks -- by expanding banks' balance sheets with linked pairs of new deposit liabilities (the debtor's new spendable, cashable deposit account credit balance) and equal new interest-earning assets (the debtor's new interest-bearing, repayable loan account or bond debt balance).

Debtors issue interest-bearing debts and sell them to banks to get new bank deposits to spend.

Debtors pay the new bank deposits to payees, within the bank-operated payments system.

Payees create the cash money supply when we make cash withdrawals. We pay for our cash withdrawals with debits to our deposit account credit balances; and banks pay some of their deposit liability debt balances in money (currency).

Payees use the currency as our cash money supply.

Payees use commercial banks' *unpaid* balance sheet deposit liability debt balances -- our deposit account credit balances -- as our *deposit account* money supply.

Debtors owe all the deposit account credit balances back to their creditor-banks, as payment of the debtors' loan account and bond debt balances.

But debtors can't pay their loan account and bond debt balances because payees have all the deposit account credit balances.

Commercial banks use debtors' *unpaid* loan account and bond debt balances as the banks' balance sheet interest-earning assets.

"Under the old "legacy" banking system, banks made loans and funded those loans with deposit liabilities." {from the Perry Mehrling quote}

"If money is viewed simply as a tool to facilitate transactions, only those media that are readily accepted in exchange for goods, services and other assets need to be considered (as) transactions money." {from the Chicago Fed quote}

"The liabilities of banks and other depository institutions have the peculiar characteristic *that they are money*. ...The public accepts them because they are accepted as money by others." {from the textbook quote}

Mehrling described how banks *create* bank deposits (by issuing deposit liabilities to fund their bank loans).

The Chicago Fed authors, and the textbook authors, define money by what money is *used for*.

We use money as our payments media: to pay for the goods, services and assets we buy; and to get paid for the goods, services (including employees' work of all kinds) and assets we sell.

"Money" is whatever kinds of payments media people who sell stuff for money accept as money payment from people who buy the stuff and pay with money.

We use currency and bank deposits as our payments media.

Most of our payments media -- our money supply -- is bank deposits: the spendable credit balances in payees' bank deposit accounts, which exist as deposit liability debts on commercial banks' balance sheets.

Payees use commercial banks' deposit liability debts as our deposit account money supply.

Payees -- money-earners -- only got involved with debtors and their creditor-banks (who create the credit-debt money) when we accepted payment in commercial banks' deposit liability debts (bank deposits) as payment "in money".

the payments system: bank deposits and bank reserves

We pay each other bank deposits -- and our banks pay each other central bank reserves -- within the central-commercial bank-operated payments system of debiting payer account balances and crediting payee account balances.

Commercial banks debit and credit their customers' deposit account balances.

The central bank debits and credits commercial banks' reserve account balances.

Commercial banks create the spendable money supply in the form of the deposit account money supply in debtors' bank deposit accounts.

Debtors pay the new bank deposits to payees within the bank-operated payments system.

Payees create the cash money supply when we cashout some of the credit balances for payment in our banks' vault cash.

But most bank deposits are never cashed out; and most money exists as credit balances in payees' bank deposit accounts.

But payees were not paid legal tender money (currency).

Payees were paid credit-debt money: bank deposits.

Payees were paid commercial banks' deposit liability debts.

Payees are banks' deposit account customers.

Deposit account customers are creditors to our debtor-banks.

Our bank deposit account balances are our spendable, cashable money assets (deposit account credit balances) that are owed as our banks' payable money liabilities (deposit liability debt balances).

When we pay bank deposits to a payee who is a customer of a different commercial bank, our bank pays an equal amount of central bank reserves into the payee-bank's reserve account to settle the payments system payment.

We paid bank deposits -- which are commercial banks' money liabilities (deposit liabilities) into the payee-bank. So our bank has to pay an equal amount of money assets (central bank reserves) into the payee-bank's reserve account to equal the new money liabilities.

E.g. when you pay a $100 utility bill by online banking; or when you pay a merchant $100 with your debit card: your bank debits your deposit account balance -$100 to clear the payment; then the payee's bank credits the payee's bank deposit account +$100.

If the payer and payee are both customers of the same commercial bank, then no reserves are involved in the payment. The bank debits the payer's deposit account -$100 and credits the payee's deposit account +$100; and the payments system payment of $100 of bank deposits is completed. The credit-debt money -- the deposit account balance -- is now in the payee's commercial bank deposit account.

If the payer and payee are customers of different commercial banks, then to settle the payment: the central bank debits the payer-bank's reserve account balance -$100 and credits the payee-bank's reserve account balance +$100. The base money -- the reserve account balance -- is now in the payee-bank's central bank reserve account.

{Because many payments of bank deposits back and forth between customers of different banks cancel each other out: reserve accounts settlements are lagged and aggregated; not performed at the same time as our deposit account balances are debited and credited.}

Commercial banks buy currency from the central bank and pay with debits to their reserve account balances.

E.g. the central bank debits your bank's reserve account balance -$100,000, then sends an armored truck delivery of 5000 $20 banknotes to your bank's vault. Your bank stocks its cash drawers and ATMs with the banknotes.

A commercial bank's reserve account balance -- plus the cash money the bank has in its vault and cash drawers and ATMs (vault cash) -- are the commercial bank's money assets (base money; reserves; liquidity) that the bank spends when it pays its money liabilities: the bank's deposit liability debts owed to its deposit account creditors: the payees who accepted payment in commercial banks' deposit liability debts (bank deposits) as payment "in money".

Currency is still "the money": legal tender; legal money.

Commercial banks are still legally liable to cashout our deposit account credit balances -- pay their deposit liability debts in cash money -- on demand.

Commercial banks pay their money liabilities (deposit liabilities) in money (currency) when we make cash withdrawals and pay with debits to our deposit account credit balances.

The debit reduced our deposit account credit balance, which simultaneously and equally reduced the bank's deposit liability debt balance: because our credit balance and the bank's debt balance is the same credit-debt financial instrument (bank deposit) as seen from opposite sides of the bank's creditor-assets/debtor-liabilities balance sheet.

E.g. you slide your debit card into the ATM and punch Withdraw $100. Your bank electronically debits your bank deposit account balance -$100, then the ATM pays out 5 $20 banknotes: $100 of spendable currency.

The -$100 debit extinguished -- cancelled out; subtracted out of existence -- $100 of the credit-debt balance in your bank deposit account.

The bank has paid $100 of its payable money liabilities (deposit liabilities) in money; you have cashed out $100 of your cashable money assets (deposit account credit balance); and you now have the money (currency) in your pocket.

The creditor-debtor relationship is extinguished when banks pay their deposit liability debts in cash money; and our bank deposit account balance is subtracted out of existence.

Commercial banks spend their money assets (reserve account balances) settling our payments of bank deposits to payees at different banks.

And commercial banks spend their reserve account balances buying currency from the central bank to get vault cash, so the banks can pay their money liabilities in legal tender money when we make cash withdrawals.

But fractional reserve banks only have enough money assets (reserve account balances) and money (vault cash) to pay a fraction of the deposit liability debts the banks owe to their deposit account creditors: the payees who accepted payment in credit-debt balances (bank deposits) as if we were being paid money (currency).

liquidity failure

When banks suffer liquidity failure, our deposit account credit balances no longer "work" as spendable, cashable, money assets.

We can't spend our credit balances by check, online banking or debit card, because our illiquid bank has an insufficient reserve account balance (NSF) for the central bank to debit to settle the payments. So the payment attempts fail. Even though we have a sufficient deposit account balance to debit to make (clear) the payment: our deposit account balance is not debited, and the payee's deposit account balance is not credited; because our illiquid bank has no base money to settle the payment.

We can't cashout our deposit account credit balance for payment in our bank's vault cash, because our illiquid bank has no cash money "in" its vault or cash drawers or ATMs; and has no reserve account balance to debit to buy more currency from the central bank.

When commercial banks suffer liquidity failure: our deposit account credit balances become the unpayable deposit liability debt balances of illiquid and insolvent (bankrupt) debtor-banks who cannot pay the money liabilities they owe to their deposit account creditors.

So bank regulators write off our deposit account credit balances to relieve the commercial banking system of its unpayable deposit liability debts.

Like bankruptcy Trustees did in the 1930s; and like the depositor bail-ins program plans to do this time.

where is all the money?

Meanwhile, so long as debtors have not earned back and paid back and extinguished the bank deposits; and so long as bank regulators have not written them off: payees use the credit balances as our deposit account money supply.

Payees re-spend and re-invest some (about 20%) of the bank deposits: pay them to the next payees. This is the producer-consumer economy's circulating money supply, that we have in our commercial bank checking accounts and businesses' current accounts: our "paying and getting paid bank deposits" accounts. {Most of the cash money supply also remains in circulation in the producer-consumer economy's invest-earn, buy-sell, spend-earn money stream.}

Payees (people, businesses, corporations, institutions) hold some (about 60%) of the bank deposits out of circulation as our earned and accumulated financial wealth and security: our long-term commercial bank savings account balances in domestic and offshore banks. Nobody -- except the payee who owns a bank deposit account balance -- is lending, investing or spending payees' bank deposit account balances. Savers *don't* lend, invest or spend our deposit account balances. We *keep them*. Savings account balances are the non-circulating* part of the deposit account money supply.

*{Which is why the M1 measure of the *circulating* money supply includes the cash money supply (currency in circulation); and "checkable" checking account and current account balances (demand deposits); and travelers checks (a form of certified checks); but does not include savings account balances.}

And payees transfer some (about 20%) of the bank deposits out of our commercial bank deposit accounts, into our shadow bank cash accounts (brokerage accounts, investment bank accounts, etc) in the savings-funded capital markets financial system: the "shadow banking" system. The transferred balances are debited out of our commercial bank deposit account balances and credited into our shadow bank cash account balances. The cash balances circulate as payments money in the capital markets financial system, as payees' *investible* money supply.

All of the bank deposits -- the deposit account money supply -- are in the commercial bank deposit accounts and shadow bank cash accounts of the most recent payees. Until we spend or invest our bank account balances -- pay them to the next payees.

Debtors owe 100% of the deposit account money supply back to their creditor-commercial banks, as payment of the debtors' unpaid -- but still owing -- loan account debt balances and bond debts.

Repaying a bank loan, or redeeming a bank-held bond, extinguishes the deposit account credit balance, and the loan account or bond debt balance, that were created by making the bank loan or bond purchase.

But debtors can't earn back and extinguish the bank deposits, because payees are holding about 60% of the total deposit account money supply out of circulation as our long-term savings account balances; and payees are using an additional 20% of the total deposit account money supply as our shadow bank cash account balances -- our investible capital.

Bank deposits that are not being spent by the payees who now have them, cannot be earned back and extinguished by the debtors who owe them back.

Only the 20% of the deposit account money supply that we have in our "paying and getting paid bank deposits" accounts -- checking accounts and current accounts -- circulates as payments money in the producer-consumer economy's invest-earn, buy-sell, spend-earn money stream where debtors could earn back the bank deposits by getting paid for working, and by selling the stuff they produce to get paid the buyers' money-spending.

[Governments don't actually paydown their accumulated bond debts.

But government debtors get money to pay bond interest by taxing money-spending (sales taxes) and money-earning (income taxes) out of the private sector economy's spend-earn stream.]

80% of the total deposit account money supply is being held by payees outside the economy's spend-earn money stream, beyond debtors' reach to "earn it back"; or tax it back {unless governments impose a capital tax that directly debits bank deposits out of our bank accounts; and uses the taxed-back bank deposits to pay bond interest to avoid bankrupting the country by defaulting on its bond debt payments}.

creditors' uncollectable credits owed as debtors' unpayable debts

The commercial banks' "repayable bank loan and bond purchase" credit-debt creation system depends on a never-ending accelerating increase in total credit-debt: new debtors spending new bank deposits into the spend-earn stream, so old debtors can earn and extinguish some of the new deposit account credit balances to extinguish (paydown) some of their old loan account debt balances.

But debtors aren't the only payees who are earning the newly-spent bank deposits. Savers and investors are earning bank deposits out of the economy's spend-earn stream, and accumulating the bank deposits out of circulation as our savings and investible capital. Which starves the spending-driven producer-consumer economy's spend-earn stream of its circulating money supply; which starves loan account debtors of money re-spending and re-investing to earn and extinguish (and starves government debtors of money-spending and money-earning to tax).

As total credit-debt increases, debtors' total monthly loan payments increase; so new credit-debt has to increase at an accelerating rate so debtors, savers and investors -- and people and businesses who earn then re-spend and re-invest the new money -- can all earn enough of the new bank deposits.

When credit-debt growth slows or stalls, not enough new bank deposits are being spent into the spend-earn stream.

So debtors can't earn enough newly-created bank deposits to pay their money-costs of living and doing business, plus pay their bank loans and bond debts.

So debtors default on paying their debts.

When debtors can't pay their loan account and bond debts, creditor-banks can't collect their balance sheet earning assets: the debtors' loan and bond principal and interest payments.

When creditor-banks can't collect their balance sheet earning assets, "fractional reserve" debtor-banks can't pay their balance sheet deposit liability debts owed to their deposit account creditors.

The creditor-bank and the debtor-bank is the same bank.

Banks are creditors to their loan account and bond debtors; and banks are debtors to their deposit account creditors.

When debtor-banks can't pay their deposit liability debts, bank regulators write off payees' deposit account credit balances to relieve the commercial banking system of its unpayable deposit liability debts.

But not before creditor-banks have seized ownership of the "mortgaged" real economic wealth of nations:

the mortgaged assets (mainly real estate, stocks and business assets) that private sector debtors explicitly pledged as collateral security against their bank loans that the debtors spent buying or building those assets;

and the public lands and resources and infrastructure that government debtors implicitly pledged as collateral security against their bond debts that are secured by the "full faith and credit" of the government's power to get money (by collecting taxes; and by selling the public wealth at liquidation sale prices) to pay bond interest and to payout bonds as the debts mature.

Repeat this process a few times over decades and centuries and you arrive at the financial state of the world today: where 80 people own as much money and assets as the other 7.6 billion people combined.

Not because the 80 people produced as much economic wealth as the other 7.6 billion people.

But because the 80 people *acquired ownership* of the money and assets -- by monetary, financial, legal, and legislative processes.

Monetary processes: commercial banking -- money supply issuance and allocation; financial processes: shadow banking -- stock issuance and allocation; legal processes: money and banking and corporation and property laws; and legislative processes: government Acts that define and enable the legal creation of central banks, commercial banks, shadow banks, corporations, money, and property.

"Money" may be no more substantial than numbers printed on slips of paperlike material (banknotes) and numbers typed into bank deposit accounts (bank deposits).

But paying money in a buy-sell, payer-payee transaction *buys ownership* of real property (assets) that was built up by the work of billions of people.

The payer-payee part of the transaction transfers ownership of *the money* from buyers to sellers: from money-payers to money-payees.

Then periodically, the system writes off apocalyptic amounts of payees' 'money in the bank'.

And anybody who still has money that wasn't written off; or credit with a still-standing bank: can buy up all the foreclosed assets at bankruptcy liquidation auctions, cheap.

The commercial banks' private monopoly of money supply issuance systematically transfers ownership of the money and assets into ever-fewer, ever-richer hands.

And reduces everybody else to wage serfdom and debt bondage.

[Read Frederick Lewis Allen's 1935 book *The Lords of Creation*;

and Richard Franklin Pettigrew's 1922 book *Triumphant Plutocracy: The Story of American Public Life from 1870-1920*;

for detailed eye-witness accounts of the monetary (commercial banking: money issuance and allocation); financial (shadow banking: brokerage and investment bank stock issuance and allocation); and political/legal (property laws and corporation legislation); processes by which America's original "1%" acquired ownership of the economic (assets) and financial (money) wealth of the United States.

Pettigrew's title is a sarcastic allusion to the title of Andrew Carnegie's 1886 book, *Triumphant Democracy, Or, Fifty Years' March of the Republic*; in which Carnegie celebrates US robber barons' democratic right to consolidate ownership of the US industrial-commercial economy into their own hands as their private corporate monopolies.

{"Plutocracy" means rule by the rich. An economy whose productive, commercial and financial infrastructure is owned by gigantic transnational industrial, commercial, and banking corporations whose annual revenues are bigger than the annual GDP of all but a handful of the biggest countries -- corporations that are governed by a Chairman and Board of Directors and Executive Managers sitting in a boardroom; a corporate government that is appointed by the controlling owners of the corporations -- is an economic "plutocracy" that is ruled by its *owners*.}

Mark Twain and Charles Dudley Warner's 1873 book, *The Gilded Age*, provides a fictional account of the same processes (focusing on the political); and the book title gave the robber baron era its 'gilded' name.

For an updated monetary history of the United States, read Ellen Brown's 2007 book (updated in 2010), *The Web of Debt: The Shocking Truth About Our Money System And How We Can Break Free*.]

obfuscating complexification

"The study of money, above all other fields in economics, is the one in which complexity is used to disguise truth or to evade truth, not to reveal it.

The process by which banks create money is so simple that the mind is repelled. Where something so important is involved, a deeper mystery seems only decent." {John K Galbraith, *Money: Whence it Came, Where it Went* (1975)}

Commercial banks create the deposit account money supply by typing numbers (bank deposits: e.g. +$1000) into the Credits column of debtors' bank deposit accounts: to "fund" the banks' loans to private sector debtors; and to fund the banks' bond purchases from government debtors. The credits add to the debtors' spendable bank deposit account *balances*.

"This means banks can create book money just by making an accounting entry." {from the Bundesbank quote}

Commercial banks create loan account and bond debts by typing equal negative numbers (-$1000: debt balances) into the debtors' bank loan and bond accounts.

Is your mind "repelled" when you see how commercial banks create the deposit account money supply, and the loan account and bond debts -- of people, businesses and nations -- by typing numbers into bank accounts?

Central bank reserves are numbers (reserve account *balances*) in commercial banks' central bank reserve accounts; in the same way bank deposits are numbers in payees' commercial bank deposit accounts.

Central banks create reserve account balances (base money) in the same way commercial banks create deposit account balances (spendable money): "by typing".

The account balances are paid out (spent, invested, or transferred into different bank accounts) by debiting payer account balances; and the account balances are paid in by crediting payee account balances.

The account balances are cashed out when commercial banks make cash withdrawals from their reserve accounts and pay with debits to their reserve account balances; and when payees make cash withdrawals from our deposit accounts and pay with debits to our deposit account balances.

The debits extinguish the banks' payable money liabilities (the central bank's reserve liabilities; commercial banks' deposit liabilities): when banks pay their money liabilities in money: banknotes and coins -- currency.

"Cash withdrawals" is a misleading term that seems to imply that account balances are originally created by making "cash deposits" in banks; which implies that we have cash money "on deposit" in our banks' vaults.

We don't.

We have numbers -- balances -- in our bank accounts.

Monetary system institutions -- central banks and commercial banks -- create bank account money (reserve account balances and deposit account balances) "by typing".

Shadow banks do not create any money. Shadow banks are financial intermediaries who get money from their customers, then -- with their customers' authorization -- spend (invest) their customers' cash account balances buying income-generating assets like stocks, bonds and money market funds.

Shadow banks create derivative creditor-assets/debtor-liabilities (like credit default swaps, interest rate swaps, and more exotic credit-debt instruments) that commercial banks and shadow banks trade ("swap") with each other in the commercial-shadow banking system. But shadow banks do not create any spendable money that can be spent buying stuff in the "real" producer-consumer economy.

Beneath the mystifying veils of Rube Goldberg monetary mechanisms and arcane financial terminology, the money system is simple.

But "money" has been complexified, so most people don't see the simple underlying reality that commercial banks create the money supply by making repayable loans of newly-created bank deposits to loan account and bond debtors.

And the banks' "repayable bank loan and bond purchase" deposit account money supply creation monopoly *doesn't work*.

It fails, and writes off our 'money in the bank'.

But that simple reality is disguised behind the mystifying veils of obfuscating complexification that surround "money".

asset-secured credit-debt creation

Most bank credit is created to finance debtors' purchases of "mortgageable" assets: stocks in the 1920s; real estate in the 2000s.

Banks purchase the debtors' new interest-bearing promissory notes -- margin notes for stocks; mortgage notes for real estate -- as the banks' interest-earning assets.

Banks purchase the mortgaged stocks and real estate as the banks' collateral assets: the banks' security against the debtors' failure to pay loan interest; and to repay the loan principal as the debts come due for payment.

If debtors default on repaying the bank deposits: banks foreclose -- seize ownership of the mortgaged collateral assets; then sell the assets to get loan-loss capital paid into the banks' own bank deposit accounts -- paid in by debiting the bank deposits out of the asset-buyers' bank deposit account balances, and credited into the asset-selling banks' own bank deposit account balances.

Then the banks write off loan-loss capital from the liability side of their balance sheets, to write off an equal amount of defaulted earning assets (loan losses) from the asset side of their balance sheets.

So instead of the debtor earning back the bank deposits -- bank deposits that are paid into the debtors' bank deposit account out of other payers' bank deposit accounts; then the debtor extinguishing the bank deposits to extinguish the debt: the creditor-bank earns the bank deposits by selling the collateral assets; then the bank extinguishes its own bank deposit account balance to extinguish the defaulted debt balance.

Debtors' interest-bearing loan account debt balances (banks' earning assets); and the sellable price of the mortgaged stocks or real estate (banks' collateral assets): are on the asset side of banks' balance sheets.

The bank deposits (deposit liabilities) that a bank originally created to fund its bank loan to the margin debtor or mortgage debtor, is on the liability side of banks' balance sheets.

Balance sheet expansion creates deposit account credit balances and equal loan account debt balances.

Balance sheet reduction extinguishes the deposit account credit balances and the loan account debt balances.

The deposit account credits and loan account debts that are created by making bank loans, must be equally extinguished to keep banks' balance sheets balanced: either by debtors earning back the bank deposits and repaying the loans; or by creditor-banks earning back the bank deposits and repaying the loans.

asset price inflation-deflation

When asset prices are stable, most owners of stocks and real estate are happy to keep their assets.

But when asset prices are increasing, asset-owners are motivated to sell their assets for more money than they paid to buy them, in order to earn money as capital gains.

Creating new buy-money in debtors' bank deposit accounts enables asset-owners to sell their assets at inflated prices to the mortgage-debtors.

The commercial banks' asset-secured bank loan money supply creation system systematically inflates asset prices.

Savers -- people who have money: people who have earned and frugally saved up bank deposit account balances -- do not typically spend their money buying assets at inflated prices. Savers are typically the same people who *already own* the stocks and houses.

But people who have no money at all, and who see the price of stocks or houses inflating, are willing to take on (what should be terrifying amounts of) loan account debt to buy into the price-inflating asset market.

As long as the sellable price of assets continues to increase, debtors can sell their mortgaged assets for more money tomorrow than they paid today. So they can payout their bank loans and earn a nice capital gain for their efforts.

Other people simply fear that ongoing asset price inflation will permanently price them out of the market, so they take the plunge into mortgage debt.

Bankers -- who also see the sellable price of assets inflating -- feel their high-ratio margin loans and mortgage loans are well-secured by the inflating sellable price of the mortgaged collateral assets.

If debtors default on paying the banks' earning assets (the debtors' loan principal and interest payments), banks can foreclose and *sell* the collateral assets to get loan loss capital paid into the banks' own bank deposit accounts by the buyers of the foreclosed-and-sold assets. Then the banks can write off the defaulted earning assets (loan losses) by writing down an equal amount of loan loss capital (writing off the bank deposits).

So debtors and their creditor-banks continue adding new deposit account buy-money into the assets-for-sale market, and the sellable price of the assets continues inflating.

Finally some shock -- $550,000 for a 30 year old Las Vegas bungalow that the owner bought new in 1975 for $30,000?! No way!!! -- pops the perceptual bubble of never-ending asset price inflation.

The bank loan (debt-financed) demand to buy assets evaporates. Buyers are not willing to borrow and spend, and banks are not willing to create and lend, new deposit account buy-money.

The credit-fueled frenzy to buy price-inflating assets turns to debt-bedraggled desperation to sell assets to get money to payout loan account debts.

But for debtors to sell assets, buyers have to buy the assets.

Savers -- people who have money -- are not going to buy the assets at those inflated prices. Savers are typically the same people who owned and lived in the 30 year old Las Vegas bungalows, and who sold their houses at inflated prices to the mortgage debtors.

House sellers now have all those new $300,000 and $500,000 deposit account balances (debtors' borrowed and spent mortgage loans) in their payee bank deposit accounts. And savers have no intention of spending their deposit account balances to buy back the houses at still-inflated prices.

When debtors and their creditor-banks stop adding new deposit account buy-money into the assets-for-sale markets, there is **no demand** -- no cash demand from savers; no debt-financed demand from new mortgage debtors -- to buy assets at those inflated prices.

So heavily-indebted asset owners drop their ask price, and drop it again, and again -- in a futile effort to get *some* money to pay at least some of their bankrupting burden of mortgage debt.

But when credit-fueled boom turns to debt-burdened bust, there are no buyers, only sellers.

The sellable price of assets *deflates*.

credit-fueled prosperity...

Adding $trillions of new deposit account credit-spending into the economy's spend-earn stream and into payees' bank deposit account balances does not *only* inflate the sellable price of the supply of already-existing assets like houses.

The productive economy -- businesses, workers, suppliers -- goes to work building more houses to sell into the demand-rich, price inflating real estate market.

Fee-collecting municipalities, real estate developers, construction companies and trade contractors, home furnishing businesses -- and all of their architects and engineers and workers and suppliers -- are among the first payees of all the $trillions of new bank deposits that are being created as bank loans and borrowed by debtors and spent into the producer-consumer economy's buy-sell, spend-earn, payer-payee money stream.

The first payees re-spend some of their new sales revenues and service fees and earned incomes and windfall capital gains buying all kinds of goods and services and assets, which creates secondary and tertiary markets to produce goods and provide services for sale. Which adds some secondary CPI price inflation.

[And which inflates the sellable *price* of the existing supply of financial assets like stocks and bonds, when newly-enriched payees transfer some of their deposit account profits, earned incomes and capital gains into their brokerage accounts to "invest" their newly-acquired financial wealth buying income-generating financial assets.

Inflating the buy-sell *price* of financial assets reduces the *yield* of those financial assets, in inverse proportion.

Asset prices today are at historic highs; and asset yields are at historic lows.

But asset price inflation creates opportunities to earn capital gains by *selling* your stocks and bonds at inflated prices. Then you sit on your cash balance and wait for asset prices to deflate so you can buy back -- at deflated prices -- the same assets you sold at inflated prices. So you have all your financial assets again. But now you also have the capital gains money.

Most people "like" assets when their price is inflating, and "don't like" assets when their price is deflating. People buy assets that they like, and sell assets that they don't like.

Most people (who get poorer) buy assets at high (inflating) prices and sell assets at low (deflating) prices. A few people (who get richer) buy low, sell high, then buy low again. Which is why a few people end up owning most of the income-generating assets and most of the investible money.]

Creating $trillions of new spendable bank deposits generates a period of spending-driven economic prosperity; and savings-inflating, asset price-inflating financial prosperity.

The productive economy is busy working and producing stuff to sell, to earn all the new bank deposits that are being created and spent and re-spent; invested and re-invested.

Payees are re-spending and re-investing some of their earnings back into the producer-consumer economy's payer-payee money stream. And payees are earning and accumulating bank account savings and brokerage account capital.

Asset *sellers* are getting richer in bank deposit account balances and brokerage account cash balances.

Asset *owners* are feeling richer about the high and rising paper prices of their real estate assets and financial assets.

Credit-fueled economic and financial prosperity is a good thing.

It's the debt-deflation downside that's the bad thing.

...turns to debt-deflation bust

When debtors and their creditor-banks stop adding new deposit account credit-spending into the economy's spend-earn stream, businesses cannot *sell* the lots and houses and furnishings they were developing and building and producing. And secondary and tertiary goods producers and service providers cannot sell their wares either.

So businesses stop producing all that stuff for sale. Businesses cut back or shut down. Businesses lay off their workers and stop buying stuff from suppliers.

Scaled-down, shut-down businesses, and newly unemployed workers and suppliers, are not earning any incomes to *pay* their mortgage loan payments.

After 2006, millions of mortgage debtors defaulted on paying $trillions of mortgage loans.

$Trillions of their creditor-banks' balance sheet earning assets became *uncollectable*: "loan losses".

The sellable price of the banks' collateral assets -- the heavily mortgaged real estate -- *deflated* by $trillions.

The banks' *collectable* earning assets and *sellable* collateral assets deflated by $trillions.

But on the *other* side of banks' balance sheets -- the *payable* deposit liability side: all the people and businesses who sold stuff to the mortgage debtors still have all those $trillions of new deposit account balances in their payee bank deposit accounts (and brokerage accounts).

Those $trillions of payees' deposit account *credit* balances are their debtor-banks' $trillions of deposit liability *debt* balances.

The collectable and sellable *asset* side of banks' balance sheets has deflated by $trillions.

But the payable deposit *liability* side of banks' balance sheets has not deflated.

Banks' owe $trillions more payable-in-cash deposit liability debts than banks have collectable earning assets and sellable collateral assets to get money to pay their deposit liability debts.

Some individual banks may be solvent.

But the commercial banking *system's* balance sheet is trillions-below-$0 *insolvent*.

bankruptcy

After the credit-inflated 1920s stock price bubble peaked and deflated, margin debtors and their creditor-banks suffered $billions of asset losses.

Banks' balance sheet earning assets -- the debtors' defaulted margin loans -- deflated by $billions.

The sellable price of the banks' balance sheet collateral assets -- the mortgaged stocks -- deflated by $billions.

But on the other side of banks' balance sheets -- the deposit liability side -- all the people who had sold stocks to the margin debtors had those new $billions of bank deposits in their payee bank deposit accounts.

Which are the banks' $billions of payable-in-cash balance sheet deposit liability debts.

When a bank's payable deposit liability debts far exceed the bank's collectable earning assets and sellable collateral assets, the bank's balance sheet is *insolvent*.

Banks' balance sheets were billions-below-$0 insolvent.

In the 1930s, illiquid and insolvent (bankrupt) banks were formally bankrupted: taken into receivership for orderly selling of their assets and paying of their liabilities.

But during a financial crisis -- a monetary-banking system failure -- money is in short supply; and there is an excess supply of goods, services and assets for sale by people who need to sell stuff to get money. So the sellable price of goods, services and assets deflates. So the bankrupt banks' assets were sold at bankruptcy liquidation auctions, cheap.

Bankruptcy Trustees paid the money -- earned by selling the bankrupt banks' assets -- to the banks' "senior" secured creditors.

When it came time to pay the banks' *unsecured* creditors -- their deposit account customers -- there was no money left.

So bankruptcy Trustees simply wrote off $billions of people's and businesses' bank deposit account balances as the unpayable deposit liability debts of bankrupt banks who could not pay the money liabilities they owed to their unsecured creditors -- the payees who had accepted payment in commercial banks' deposit liability debts as if they were being paid "money".

Solvency was restored to the commercial banking *system* by bankrupting 1000s of individual banks out of the credit-debt creation business; and by writing off $billions of the banking *system's* unpayable deposit liability debts.

The still-standing banks bought up the bankrupt banks' assets (performing loans and collateral assets) for pennies on the dollar.

The consolidation process has continued, and banks are now far bigger and far fewer than the 1930s.

After the credit-inflated 2000s real estate price bubble peaked and deflated, mortgage debtors and their creditor-banks suffered $trillions of asset losses.

This time banks' balance sheets are trillions-below-$0 insolvent, which is 1000 times worse than the billions-below-$0 insolvency during the 1930s banking system Collapse.

In 2009, Kansas City Fed President Thomas Hoenig published *Too Big Has Failed* (pdf online), in which he advocated taking the technically bankrupt banks into receivership for orderly selling of their assets and payment of their liabilities; then breaking them up into much smaller and more numerous banks and putting them back in business under new management.

But too big to fail proved to be too politically and financially powerful to regulate, so none of the banks were formally bankrupted.

The 1999 Gramm-Leach-Bliley Act repealed the 1933 Glass-Steagall Act that had prevented deposit-creating commercial banks and deposit-taking shadow banks from owning each other; or from being owned by the same controlling shareholders and "senior" creditors.

Some commercial banks now own their own brokerages and investment banks; and some brokerages and investment banks now own their own commercial banks that have access to central bank-issued base money ("liquidity": reserve account balances and vault cash), and the central-commercial bank-operated payments system.

Deposits in commercial banks are partially protected by deposit insurance, and by the possibility of central bank liquidity injections.

Deposits in shadow banks are subject to unprotected losses.

Commercial banks are now too interconnected to fail individually, and bound into derivative creditor-debtor relationships (like credit default swaps) with shadow banks.

Shadow banks have been declared "supersenior" creditors to their commercial bank derivative counterparties. Supersenior means shadow banks bet paid *first,* if commercial banks are formally bankrupted and their assets are sold to get money to pay their creditors.

Deposit account customers are "superjunior" *unsecured* creditors to our debtor-banks. Unsecured means we get paid *last,* if there is any money left to pay us at all, after shadow bank derivative counterparties have been paid.

Which there won't be (any money left to pay us).

Commercial banks' derivative downside liability is multiple times bigger than the deposit liability debts commercial banks owe to their unsecured deposit account customers.

So if the commercial banks are formally bankrupted, all of their assets simply get transferred into the waiting arms of their co-owned or partner shadow banks.

The shadow banking system would *replace* the commercial banking system: by writing off the commercial banks' unpayable deposit liability debts; and by acquiring ownership of all the bankrupt commercial banks' assets.

Commercial banks would have no collectable, sellable assets left to get money to pay their deposit liabilities.

And payees' commercial bank deposit account balances would be reduced to worthless numbers in extinct accounts, just like 1930s deposit account customers' credit balances in their bankrupt banks.

extraordinary measures

Since the 2008 banking system failure: "extraordinary" fiscal policies (giving taxpayers' money to failed banks); monetary policies (QE that adds reserves into illiquid banks' reserve accounts); and regulatory policies (regulatory forbearance that does not require insolvent banks to "recognize" their balance sheet insolvency; which would require resolution by bank bankruptcies, like the 1930s); have been keeping the technically bankrupt (illiquid and insolvent) commercial banking system in the credit-debt money supply creation business.

Under QE (quantitative easing) programs: the central bank adds reserves into commercial banks' reserve accounts to prevent banks from involuntarily defaulting on paying their deposit liability debts.

QE can and does prevent banking system liquidity failure.

QE is a new innovation that wasn't available in the 1930s when central bank reserve creation was limited by the amount of gold the central bank had in its vault.

The gold standard: fractional 'gold-backing' -- of commercial bank-issued bank deposits (credit-debt money); of central bank-issued bank reserves (base money); and of central bank-issued banknotes (paper currency) -- has been abandoned, and central banks can now create unlimited amounts of reserve account balances and vault cash (base money) for commercial banks.

QE is the reason our 'money in the bank' has not already been written off.

But restoring liquidity to illiquid banks' reserve accounts does not restore solvency to insolvent banks' balance sheets.

That's the problem debt-for-equity swaps (depositor bail-ins) will solve: by bailing-in and writing off $trillions of our bank deposit account balances to relieve the commercial banking system of $trillions of its unpayable deposit liability debts.

Writing off our 'money in the bank' is the business-as-usual solvency restoration program, after a period of credit-inflated prosperity (1914-1929; 1939-2008) turns to debt-deflation bust.

The commercial banks' debt-based credit-debt money supply creation monopoly is arithmetically incapable of generating any other outcome.

A monetary system that creates the money supply as repayable loans to debtors, is arithmetically incapable of accommodating payees earning and accumulating the money as our circulating payments media (our commercial bank checking account balances and businesses' current account balances); our financial wealth and security (our commercial bank savings account balances); and our investible capital (our shadow bank cash account balances).

Debtors owe it all back.

But debtors can't pay their loan account and bond debts because payees have all the deposit account *money*.

Extraordinary measures have been keeping the failed banks in the credit-debt creation business.

But the commercial banks' monopoly of money supply issuance has not changed.

And the banks' creation of ever-increasing totals of debtors' unpayable debt balances and creditors' uncollectable credit balances has not changed.

The credit-debt expansion has been kept limping along.

Between 2006-2017, total US government bond debt doubled from $9.5 trillion to $19 trillion; and is still increasing at a rapid rate.

Since 2010, banks have renewed "sub-prime" lending to private sector debtors -- students (student loans), car buyers (car loans), and house buyers (again: mortgage loans) -- who cannot possibly repay their $trillions of new bank loans out of their minimal or non-existent earned incomes. Up to 1/3 of all those new loans are delinquent or defaulting or defaulted: debtors have no money to pay their debts, so debtors aren't making their bank loan payments; so creditor-banks aren't collecting their balance sheet earning assets.

But payees -- people who sold college educations and cars and real estate to all the debtors -- now have all those $trillions of new bank deposits in their payee bank deposit accounts. Which are the commercial banks' new $trillions of unpayable deposit liability debts.

The kind of extraordinary measure that would actually solve the problem: QE for the economy -- government issuance of debt-free money; paid into every citizen's bank deposit account as a monthly un-earned income; so banks could debit debtors' delinquent and defaulting loan payments out of the debtors' bank deposit account balances; so banks could collect their earning assets and pay their deposit liabilities -- is not being done.

So the next mass debtor default, Collapse of the banks' credit-debt money system, writeoff of our bank deposit account balances, $trillions of creditor and investor money and asset losses, and Debt-Deflation Depression: is just a matter of when, not if.

But this time our 'money in the bank' will be written off *by other means*.

debt-for-equity

After the 2008-09 bailout debacle, the 2010 Dodd-Frank legislation vowed, No more taxpayer money to bailout banks!

G20 (and other national) monetary authorities have signed onto Dodd-Frank's debt-for-equity swaps program: depositor bail-ins.

So this time, instead of bailing out the banking *system* in your role as a taxpayer, you will restore solvency to your own insolvent bank in your role as a deposit account customer.

This time you're going to *feel it*.

Banks and bank regulators plan to debit $trillions of deposit account balances out of our bank deposit accounts -- and credit the payments into our banks' own bank deposit accounts -- to "pay for" the newly-issued bank shares (equity) that we are going to (involuntarily) buy.

Banks are still legally liable to cashout our deposit account credit balances -- pay their deposit liability debts in cash money -- on demand.

But banks are under no obligation to pay back the money we "invested" buying shares from the banks.

By debiting our deposit account balances to pay for our (involuntary) investment in bank shares: banks and bank regulators convert the banks' payable-in-cash deposit liability debts into non-payable shareholder equity.

"Debt-for-equity".

Instead of "having money in the bank" (which is not actually money; but at least it worked like money), we will "own shares in the bank".

A basic bank balance sheet looks like this: Assets = Capital + Liabilities.

A corporate balance sheet "balances" to $0: Assets *owned* = Capital + other Liabilities *owed* = $0.

A corporation is "property" that is *owned* by its owners -- the shareholders. Everything the corporation "has" is *owed to* the owners of the corporation.

So a corporation's net worth is reported on the *liability* side of the corporate balance sheet, as line items like shareholder equity, retained earnings, and capital.

As a share-issuing business corporation, a bank owes its net worth to its human owners -- the shareholders.

Capital is a bank's own money.

Capital, and shareholder equity, are on the liability side of the = sign.

Loan loss capital is part of a bank's capital, the bank's own money: like transferring some of your deposit account balance out of your "emergency money" savings account into your checking account, then spending your checking account balance to pay your emergency costs.

Our deposit account balances will be debited in the amount of our purchase of newly-issued bank shares; and our payments will be credited into our share-selling banks' own bank deposit accounts, as the banks' new paid-in capital. Then our banks will use our bailed-in capital as their loan loss capital.

Banks will write down $trillions of the loan loss capital on the liability side of their balance sheets, to write off equal $trillions of (mortgage) loan losses from the (uncollectable) earning asset side of their balance sheets.

$Trillions of the banks' payable-in-cash deposit liability debts -- our bailed-in deposit account credit balances -- will be *extinguished*: written off; simply subtracted out of existence by "debits".

But balance sheet solvency has not yet been restored, because the liability side of bank balance sheets is now inflated with shareholder equity liabilities.

[Stocks -- equity ownership shares in business corporations -- are financial assets. Assets are not money. Assets are bought-sold for money. To convert your assets into money, you have to sell your assets to somebody who will pay their money to buy your assets. If you can't sell your assets -- if nobody who has money will spend their money buying your assets -- how much "money" are your assets "worth"?]

Cyprus was the trial run. It worked to the banks' and regulators' satisfaction.

For a time we will not be allowed to try to sell our new bank shares. When we are finally allowed to sell our shares, we will discover that investors are not willing to pay the inflated price that we (involuntarily) paid for the shares. Vulture funds might offer us 2 cents on the dollar to buy our shares.

The realized price of shares is the price paid by a buyer to a seller.

The paper "market" price of all the still un-sold shares is established by the most recent actual buy-sell price of shares.

When bailed-in shareholders -- desperate to convert their financial assets into spendable money that they need -- start selling their shares at low prices, the market price of *all of* the bank shares will *deflate*.

The asset side of bank balance sheets will have already been deflated by writing off $trillions of uncollectable earning assets as loan losses, paid down by writing off equal $trillions of our bailed-in loan loss capital.

But the liability side of bank balance sheets was still inflated with the inflated prices we paid for bank shares, which added to shareholders' equity, which is banks' balance sheet shareholder liability.

The balance sheet is still unbalanced: Assets are *less than* Capital + Liabilities.

Balance sheet solvency: Assets = Capital + Liabilities; will finally be achieved when banks' shareholder liability deflates.

Debt-for-equity swaps restore solvency to bank balance sheets by selling us worthless shares in insolvent banks then extinguishing (writing off) $trillions of what used to be our deposit account 'money' supply.

Banks and bank regulators plan to extinguish $trillions of our spendable bank deposit account balances, and plunge the spending-driven producer-consumer economy into the mother of all Debt-Deflation Depressions, to solve the banks' balance sheet arithmetic problem.

This is not an anomaly.

The commercial banks' repayable bank loan money supply creation monopoly is arithmetically incapable of generating any other outcome.

After a credit-inflated asset price bubble -- and the associated spending-driven economic boom -- peaks and deflates: debtors and their creditor-banks suffer bankrupting asset losses; and the commercial banking system's structural insolvency is exposed when debtor-banks suffer liquidity failure and can't pay their balance sheet deposit liability debts.

QE to prevent banking system liquidity failure is a new innovation.

Writing off our deposit account credit balances to relieve the commercial banking system of its unpayable deposit liability debts is the business-as-usual solvency restoration program.

Depositor bail-ins are debtor-banks *defaulting* -- by other means -- on *paying* the deposit liability debts the banks owe to "us" -- the banks' deposit account creditors: the payees who accepted payment in bank deposits as payment "in money".

The Dodd-Frank debt-for-equity swaps will be the biggest debtor default in the history of credit-debt financial instruments that are not "money".

money liabilities (account balances) and money (currency)

"Banking" is the business or institution of issuing money liabilities (banks' debts) to purchase interest-earning assets (debtors' loan account and bond debts).

The central bank is a "bank".

The central bank issues reserve liabilities (reserve account balances) in the same way commercial banks issue deposit liabilities (deposit account balances).

"The liabilities of banks...have the peculiar characteristic that they are money."

The central bank's reserve liabilities -- which are commercial banks' reserve account balances -- are base money: commercial banks' money assets that are owed as the central bank's money liabilities.

Commercial banks' deposit liabilities -- which are customers' deposit account balances -- are spendable money: customers' money assets that are owed as commercial banks' money liabilities.

The money assets are collectable, and the money liabilities are payable, in money: currency.

The central bank can always pay its money liabilities (reserve liabilities) in money (currency), because the central bank *issues the money*: the currency.

The central bank issues *non-defaultable* money liabilities: reserve account balances. Commercial banks can always cashout their reserve account balances to get vault cash, because the central bank can always pay the money, because the central bank issues the currency: the money.

Unlike commercial banks who issue defaultable money liabilities: deposit account balances.

Commercial banks can and do run out of money assets (reserve account balances) and money (vault cash) and default on paying their deposit liability debts.

Which is why central bank-issued reserve account balances and currency are equally "the money".

Whereas commercial bank-issued deposit account balances are defaultable credit-debt instruments.

"risk-free" government debt and base money creation

The central bank creates base money (reserve account balances) in commercial banks' reserve accounts when the central bank buys interest-earning debt-assets (mainly government bond debts) from commercial banks, and pays with money-assets: central bank reserves.

The central bank pays for its asset purchases by typing numbers (central bank reserves) into the Credits column of the bond-selling commercial banks' reserve accounts. The credits add to the commercial banks' reserve account *balances*.

That's where central bank reserves come from. The central bank creates reserve account balances "by typing".

Commercial banks "get bonds" by purchasing new issues of interest-bearing Treasury bills, notes, bonds -- government bond debts -- from the government. Commercial banks pay for their purchases of those interest-earning debt-assets by typing numbers (bank deposits) into the Credits column of the bond-selling government's commercial bank deposit accounts. The credits add to the government's spendable bank deposit account *balances*.

That's where governments get their deficit-spending money. Commercial banks create spendable deposit account balances "by typing".

The government typically transfers the bond-sale credits out of its commercial bank deposit accounts, into its central bank account; then spends the credits out of its central bank account, paid into payees' (government spending recipients) commercial bank deposit accounts. The central bank debits the payment amounts out of the government's central bank account balance; and the payees' commercial banks credit the payment amounts into the payees' commercial bank deposit account balances.

Government bond debt is considered a "risk-free" banking system asset -- free of default risk: assuming the government can always get money to pay its debts by taxing money spending (sales taxes) and money-earning (income taxes) out of the private sector economy's spend-earn stream; and by selling the public lands and resources and infrastructure (at debt-distressed prices far below the amount taxpayers paid to build the public infrastructure) to get money to pay bond interest, and to payout the bonds as they mature and the debt comes due for repayment.

Under QE (quantitative easing) programs, central banks are buying risk-assets {like MBS: mortgage-backed securities -- securitized bundles of private debtors' defaulting mortgage loan debts; and CDOs: collateralized debt obligations -- securitized bundles of private debtors' defaulting car loans and other consumer debts} off commercial banks' balance sheets; and replacing the defaulting interest-earning debt-assets with non-defaultable money assets: reserve account balances.

Commercial banks issue deposit liabilities (deposit account balances) to pay for their purchases of new issues of government debt.

The central bank issues reserve liabilities (reserve account balances) to pay for its purchases of interest-earning debt-assets from commercial banks.

The primary dealer commercial banks -- who create new bank deposits to pay for their purchases of the government's new bond debts -- typically sell most of the government's debts into the secondary markets: the capital markets where central banks buy-sell bonds to conduct their interest rate-influencing open market monetary policy operations; and where non-primary dealer commercial banks buy bonds to hold on their balance sheets as interest-earning assets, and as their near-money capital, and to sell to the central bank to get reserves in their reserve accounts; and where shadow banks buy bonds to hold as "risk-free" collateral (e.g. repurchase agreements) against all kinds of derivative credit-debt creation; and where you -- and your pension fund and insurance company and mutual fund -- buy bonds to hold as interest-paying financial assets in your brokerage accounts.

"Risk-free" interest-bearing Treasury debt provides the stable base of the central-commercial banks' money and credit-debt creation system.

And interest-paying government bond debt -- the bond market -- is by far the capital markets biggest class of income-generating financial assets.

[Stocks -- dividend-paying equity ownership shares in business corporations -- are a distant second biggest class of financial assets.

But stocks (the stock market) and bonds (the bond market) are dwarfed by real estate (the real estate market).

Real estate is by far the biggest asset class -- and the biggest class of mortgageable assets to pledge as collateral security against mortgage loans -- in every economy.

But not all real estate is mortgaged, and today total government bond debt is bigger than total private sector mortgage debt.

And because of the government's power to get money to pay its debts -- by taxing and by selling the public wealth -- interest-paying government bond debt is a more "secure" banking system asset than private debtors' mortgage debts.]

ever-increasing total debt

Governments don't actually paydown their total accumulated bond debts.

Governments roll over their maturing bonds: sell new bonds to (primary dealer) commercial banks who create new bank deposits in the government's bank deposit accounts which the government spends to payout old bonds as payment comes due.

And governments add to the total public debt year after year by issuing more new bond debts than they payout old bond debts.

Which is why total US Treasury debt has increased from $0 in 1835 when Andrew Jackson paid off the national debt, to $90 million before the Civil War and $2.7 billion after the Civil War, to $24 billion during WWI, to $259 billion during WWII, to $1 trillion by 1981, to $9.5 trillion in 2006, to nearly $19 trillion in 2017.

Total US Treasury debt before the Civil War was only $90 million.

Despite Lincoln's printing of $450 million of debt-free, interest-free United States Notes (greenbacks) to pay some of the North's Civil War costs in government-issued legal tender money, total US Treasury debt after the Civil War was $2.7 billion.

Which is a 30X increase in total government bond debt over the 4 years (April 12, 1861 - May 9, 1865) of the Civil War.

The debt is **never** paid down.

A *permanent* 5-10X increase in total "public debt" is typical of bond debt-financed War spending.

[Read Smedley Butler's 1935 booklet, *War is a Racket*, to see who *profits* from War.]

If you had told Teddy Roosevelt in 1909 -- after total US Treasury debt had remained fairly stable at $2.7 billion since 1865 -- that total US government bond debt would grow 7000 times bigger over the next 108 years -- from $2.7 billion in 1909 to $19 trillion in 2017: Roosevelt would have laughed you out of the Oval Office.
Yet, here we are.

And total US private sector loan account debt has increased by more than 10,000 times over the same period.

The private sector as a whole doesn't paydown its total loan account debt, just like the government sector doesn't paydown its total bond debt.

Some loan account debtors are always earning bank deposits out of the spend-earn stream and extinguishing the credit balances to extinguish (paydown) their debt balances. But new debtors are borrowing and spending new bank deposits into the spend-earn stream at the same time. New debtors are adding more new bank deposits, than old debtors are paying back and extinguishing old bank deposits.

Within the commercial banks' "repayable bank loan and bond purchase" money supply creation system: banks create the new money to purchase the new debts.

Repaying the debts un-creates the money.

A growing buy-sell for money economy requires an expanding circulating money supply to accommodate the increased volume of buy-sell transactions. Meanwhile, payees are earning money out of the spend-earn stream then holding it out of circulation as our accumulations of bank account savings and brokerage account capital.

For people's checking account balances and businesses' current account balances (the circulating money supply) to increase; for savers' commercial bank savings account balances to increase; for capital markets investors' shadow bank cash account balances to increase: debtors' loan account and bond debt balances have to equally increase and stay increased, **forever**.

But eventually interest payments on the $trillions of accumulated debts consume so much of people's earned incomes, businesses' sales revenues, and governments' tax receipts: that debtors default en masse and the commercial banks' zero-sum balance sheet money supply creation system Collapses in a smouldering heap of arithmetic impossibilities.

governments issue debts, not money

The government's role in the monetary system is to issue the banking system's supply of "risk-free" interest-earning debt-assets: "securities" -- government bond debts.

The monetary system -- the central-commercial bank money and credit-debt creation system -- is built on a foundation of government-issued debt; not government-issued money.

In US$ and in US$ equivalent in all other currencies (euros, pounds, yen, yuan, rubles, etc), the banking system has created a global total of about $100 trillion of bank deposits and currency as the world's money supply.

Ever-increasing totals of "risk-free" government bond debt forms the stable base of the banks' debt-based money supply creation system.

Which is why every government on Earth is a billionaire or trillionaire bond-debtor; not a rich-as-Midas money-printer.

credit-debt expansion then Collapse

The commercial banks' "repayable bank loan and bond purchase" deposit account credit-debt creation system depends on a never-ending accelerating increase in total credit-debt.

When credit-debt growth slows or stalls, debtors default en masse; which evaporates the illusion that the unpayable debts are somehow payable; and the uncollectable credits are somehow collectable.

So banking system regulators write off all the uncollectable credits and unpayable debts in mass credit-debt writedown events.

As long as total credit-debt continues increasing at a fast enough rate, the commercial banks' credit-debt money supply creation system appears to "work".

So the money problem -- and monetary system reform -- were forgotten during the decades since the present credit-debt expansion began in 1939 with bond debt-financed World War 2.

It is only when the system fails that people begin to look at the monetary system -- the money supply creation (and un-creation) system -- to see how it works.

Since the 1920s, monetary macroeconomists -- people who look at the money system -- have clearly described why the commercial banks' debt-based money supply creation monopoly *doesn't work*.

And since the 1930s a succession of monetary system reformers have advocated a variety of simple and viable ways to fix the money system.

All of these monetary system reformers advocate government issuance of debt-free (non-repayable; non-extinguishable) money; as a solution to the built-in failings of the commercial banks' zero-sum credit-debt creation system.

A debt-free money supply can be earned and accumulated by payees without making debtors' debts unpayable, banks' earning assets uncollectable, banks' deposit liability debts unpayable, and payees' deposit account credit balances uncollectable.

But no reforms have ever been implemented.

The banks' monopoly of credit-debt money supply issuance has not changed.

So the next banking system failure -- and writeoff of $trillions of our deposit account credit balances -- is a matter of when, not if, it is going to happen.

It doesn't have to be this way.

Governments could create debt-free digital money "by typing"; in the same way commercial banks create digital credit-debt money by typing; and central banks create digital base money by typing.

Debtors could pay their debts with the new money; instead of the impossible task of earning back and extinguishing the old bank deposits that savers and investors now have and are not spending.

The commercial banks' debt-based credit-debt creation system could be *fixed*, simply by adding debt-free money into the credit-debt money supply.

Commercial banking -- creating deposit account credits to purchase loan account debts -- is not the problem.

The commercial banks' *monopoly of money supply issuance* is the problem.

the commercial banking system should be fixed, not replaced

Bank deposits are a highly convenient and secure form of electronic payments money (digital money). A buyer anywhere on Earth, can pay a seller anywhere else on Earth, instantaneously, within the globally-integrated bank-operated electronic payments system.

The payments system processes 100s of millions of transactions every day.

Transaction fees are so small that a global merchant like Apple can sell iTunes songs for 99 cents, without transaction fees eating up all the sales revenues and profits.

The modern global buy-sell for money economy could not function without credit-allocating and debt-collecting bankers, banks, digital bank account money, and the bank-operated payments system.

Virtually all of the world's money supply exists as deposit liabilities on banks' balance sheets.

Which is why failure of the commercial banking system is catastrophic for the money-using world.

Which is why the banks' money system should be fixed (by adding debt-free government-issued money into the commercial bank-issued deposit account money supply; and adding equal new central bank reserves into commercial banks' reserve accounts), rather than allowed to fail, then replaced with something that is worse.

But most people believe we *already have* a government-issued money system, and a financial intermediary banking system; or they believe the productive economy produces the money by producing stuff that has tradeable exchange value: so they don't understand what possible *difference* these revolutionary monetary system reforms would make.

I hope this book describes the banks' credit-debt creation system in clear enough terms to dispel those popular misconceptions out of people's minds, and replace them with seeing how the monetary-financial system actually works.

Seeing how the banks' credit-debt creation system works, exposes why it fails, and illuminates the technically simple way to fix it; add positive sums of debt-free money into the zero-sum credit-debt money supply.

popular misconceptions

Every nation on Earth uses the same commercial bank-issued "repayable bank loan and bond purchase" deposit account money supply creation system, and cash withdrawal system, and has been for a very long time.

Every government on Earth is a billionaire or trillionaire bond-debtor; not a rich-as-Midas money-printer.

Everybody *knows* that.

In the "50 years ago today" section of daily newspapers, headlines warn of Fiscal Crisis!!! and alarming and unsustainable levels of government debt.

Government *debt* is front page news, everywhere, and has been for a very long time.

But most people -- no less today than when Irving Fisher published *100% Money and the Public Debt* in 1936 -- continue to believe the government issues *the money*.

People believe they have government-issued money "on deposit" in their banks' vaults.

People believe "deposit money is genuine money in trust".

In the 1930s, when bankruptcy Trustees wrote off $billions of people's and businesses' deposit account balances in their bankrupt banks, people were astonished. Where did all our *money* go?!

But then -- as now -- we do not have legal tender currency on deposit in our banks' vaults.

We have commercial banks' deposit liability debts in our bank deposit accounts.

And when commercial banks can't pay their deposit liability debts, monetary regulators write off our 'money in the bank'.

In the 1930s, a billion was a lot of money.

Fisher identified the bankruptcy writeoff of 8 billions dollars of bankrupt banks' unpayable deposit liability debts -- over one third of payees' "checkbook money" -- as the direct cause of the 1930s Debt-Deflation Depression.

Debt-Deflation Depression is not caused by debtors defaulting on paying their unpayable bank loans and bond debts.

That just bankrupts creditor-banks.

Debt-Deflation Depression is caused by debtor-banks defaulting on paying their unpayable deposit liability debts -- payees' bank deposit account balances -- payees' spendable deposit account *money supply*.

monetary system reform

Irving Fisher's radical monetary system reform proposal -- conversion from the commercial banks' debt-based credit-debt creation system backed by the banks' holdings of fractional reserves of central bank-issued reserve account balances and vault cash; to a 100% government-issued money system and 100% reserve banking where banks get loanable funds from their depositors then lend out their depositors' savings -- would have made people's "popular misconceptions" about money, banking and credit-debt creation, *true*.

Fisher observed that people seemed happy enough with the government-issued money system and 100% reserve banking system that they believed in. So why not change the actual monetary system so that it becomes the government-issued money system people innocently but mistakenly believe they already have?

But no monetary system reforms -- radical or otherwise -- have ever been implemented.

In the 1930s about 10% of the money supply was currency and 90% bank deposits -- "check-book money".

It varies by country and currency system, but today the ratio is more like 3-5% legal tender money (currency) and 95-97% credit-debt money (bank deposits).

The commercial banks' monopoly of credit-debt money supply issuance has grown more absolute, not less, over the past century.

Most monetary system reformers -- historically and today -- are of the "radical" Irving Fisher persuasion who advocate repealing Bank Acts and revoking banks' licenses to create the bank deposits they lend, and totally replacing the banks' credit-debt creation monopoly with a 100% government-issued money creation monopoly.

Every one of these radical monetary system reform proposals has produced the same outcome: nothing changed at all. {Most recently, Swiss voters rejected conversion to a "sovereign money" issuance monopoly, in the June 10, 2018 referendum on the Vollgeld Initiative (pdf online).}

"Moderate" monetary system reformers (like Adair Turner, Steve Keen, and me) advocate *supplementing* the banks' credit-debt creation with *some* government debt-free money issuance -- as much as it takes to paydown the total debts to a realistic level and restore solvency to debtor-households and debtor-banks; then enough to serve the economy's ongoing need for a permanently increasing (non-repayable, non-extinguishable) money supply to accommodate permanently increasing savings and investible capital accumulation by payees without starving debtors of debt repayment money and without starving the producer-consumer economy of its circulating money supply.

In chapter 4 I will describe how a moderate monetary reform could be implemented, without any changes to existing monetary legislation or monetary system processes: to prevent the otherwise arithmetically inevitable banking system Collapse and writeoff of our 'money in the bank'; and without creating excessive money supply inflation that causes CPI price inflation that reduces the purchasing power of payees' already existing money supply.

Before we see how the monetary system can be fixed: let's dispel some other popular misconceptions by seeing where money *doesn't* come from.

Money is Created, Not Produced

everybody needs money

We use money every day.

You only pay once a month, but every day you are buying electricity from the electric utility, buying water from the water utility, buying service from the phone and cable and internet service provider companies. And more often than monthly, buying food from the grocer.

Most people pay monthly rent or mortgage payments. Everybody pays property taxes on their residence, either directly as property owners or included in their rent.

If you have no money to pay your bills: your electricity and water and phone and cable and internet get shut off. You can't buy food. You get evicted from your house for non-payment of your mortgage or rent or property taxes.

We cannot *live* without money.

We cannot pay our money-costs of living, unless we get money by earning money, borrowing money, or being given money.

Almost none of us directly produces any of our daily necessities of life. We don't grow our own food, build our own houses, provide our own water and fuel and electricity.

We don't live in "nature" as hunter-gatherers: we don't get our living from the land and the natural resources that the Earth provides.

We don't live in a self-sufficient peasant economy: we don't produce stuff for our own use.

We don't live in a barter exchange economy: we don't produce stuff to trade for other stuff.

Virtually everything that is produced is produced "for sale", and is sold-bought for money.

We live in a buy-sell for money producer-consumer economy, and we get our living by getting and spending money.

we do not produce or create our own money

Money is the central feature and the most basic necessity of our *economic* lives and livelihoods.

We work to get paid money. We produce stuff to sell for money. We buy everything we need and want from "the economy", and we pay with money.

We use money as our payments media: to pay for the goods, services and assets we buy; and to get paid for the goods, services and assets we sell.

We use currency (the cash money supply in our pockets) and bank deposits (the deposit account money supply in our bank accounts) as our payments media: our money supply.

But we do not produce or create our own money.

We do not go to work each day and "make money".

Free market production of spendable banknotes and coins is called "counterfeiting", which is illegal. Governments and central banks have a monopoly on issuing the currency: the legal tender money -- the cash money supply.

Free market creation of spendable bank deposit account balances is called "hacking", which is illegal. Commercial banks have a monopoly on issuing bank deposits: the credit-debt money -- the deposit account money supply.

We do not "earn money" by working and producing stuff.

As employees we earn money by getting paid money for working: paid by our employers.

As businesses we earn money by selling the stuff we produce, to get paid the buyers' money-spending.

If nobody will pay us for working; if we can't sell the stuff we produce; then we can't earn any money by working and producing stuff.

Almost all *economic* recessions/depressions are caused by monetary problems in the commercial banks' money supply creation monopoly; not by shortages of workers, suppliers, and productive businesses who put it all together into useful and necessary stuff for sale.

During depressions, the businesses and their workers and suppliers are still "there", ready to go to work producing everything that everybody needs and wants.

But the people who need to buy the stuff have no money to pay the people who need to earn money by producing and selling the stuff.

So the spending-driven producer-consumer economy just sits there doing nothing, for want of the money-spending that puts the productive economy to work producing stuff *for sale* to earn the buyers' money-spending.

2 different economies

We have 2 different kinds of economies -- a productive economy and a financial economy.

The productive economy produces goods, provides services, and builds or makes assets, for sale, for money.

Goods, services and assets are bought-sold for money in the money-using financial economy: the invest-earn, buy-sell, spend-earn, payer-payee money economy.

Neither the productive economy that *produces* stuff for sale, for money; nor the financial economy within which we *use money* to conduct all of our payer-payee money transactions; produce or create their own money.

Money is *created* by the monetary system; almost exclusively by commercial banks making repayable loans of bank deposits to loan account and bond debtors.

The debt-bound people, businesses and governments of the world cannot "produce their way out of debt": because producing more stuff for sale does not produce any new money to buy the stuff or to pay the debts.

the money system is the economy's financial nervous system

Businesses spend (invest) their cost-money paying their workers and suppliers who contribute inputs to the businesses' productive processes. Business investment of their cost-money becomes workers' and suppliers' spendable earned incomes; in invest-earn transactions.

Then in their role as consumers, workers and suppliers spend their earned incomes buying the stuff the productive businesses offer for sale; in buy-sell, spend-earn transactions.

Production (of a supply of stuff for sale) is a money *cost* to businesses, who payout (invest) their cost-money paying their workers' and suppliers' earned incomes.

Businesses earn money -- in sales revenues, service fees, rents, etc -- by selling the stuff they produce, not by producing it.

The productive economy is put to work -- driven -- by the spending of money. Consumers spending money buying stuff, puts producer-businesses and their workers/suppliers to work producing stuff for sale, to earn the buyers' money-spending.

If a business earns back in sales revenues, more money than it paid out in costs, the business earns money-profits that become the business owners' spendable incomes. "Profit" is how business owners *get paid for* their contribution to the productive process.

If a business earns less money in sales revenues than it pays out as its costs, the business suffers money losses, and the business owners soon run out of their own money to lose and are bankrupted out of the producing stuff for sale business.

Businesses' invested cost-money = workers'/suppliers' spendable earned incomes.

Governments tax and redistribute the re-spending of some of the private sector incomes; but tax-and-redistribute does not add any additional new money into the invest-earn, buy-sell, spend-earn money stream.

How can businesses earn more money *out* of the economy's spend-earn stream in sales revenues, than they invest *into* the economy's invest-earn stream as their costs -- which are workers/suppliers-cum-consumers' spendable earned incomes; in order to stay in business as money-profitable financial enterprises?

How can consumers *spend more money* buying stuff from businesses; than the amount of money consumers are paid by working for and selling stuff to businesses?

Debt.

Loan account and bond debtors spend the additional new money into the spend-earn stream, which businesses can earn as their profits, and accumulate as their investible (but not invested) capital: their commercial bank deposit account balances.

Businesses also invest their profits into the capital markets; which removes more money out of the producer-consumer economy's invest-earn, buy-sell, spend-earn money stream.

It is only debtors' ongoing spending of newly-created bank deposits into the economy's spend-earn stream that keeps the whole financial economy "liquid" with new money-spending; while payees are earning money out of the stream as our earned incomes and profits; then holding the bank deposits out of circulation as our ever-increasing totals of bank account savings and brokerage account capital.

When plenty of new money is being spent into the economy's buy-sell, spend-earn stream, businesses and their workers/suppliers go to work producing goods, providing services, and building or making assets, for sale, to earn the buyers' money-spending.

Some of the new money is re-spent and re-invested back into the economy's payer-payee money stream; but most of it is quite quickly earned and accumulated as payees' savings and investible capital. So the producer-consumer economy's payer-payee money stream depends on ongoing injections of "liquidity" -- new money -- to replace the old money that has been earned by payees who hold it out of circulation.

When little new money is being spent, businesses can't sell the stuff they produce, so businesses stop producing more stuff they can't sell.

Businesses lay off workers, stop buying stuff from suppliers, and downsize or close up shop.

Businesses stop paying out spendable earned incomes to their laid-off workers and suppliers. So consumers have even less incomes to spend, which further reduces producers' sales revenues -- and business money-profits turn to money-losses -- so producer-businesses lay off more workers/suppliers and payout even less earned incomes; in the familiar downward spiral into financial-cum-economic recession/depression.

The "real" producer-consumer economy -- the production and use/consumption of physical economic goods (food, iPads); services (water, phone, internet, legal and financial services; employees' wage, salary and contract work of all kinds); and assets (consumer assets like houses to live in and cars to drive; producer assets like land and resources and technologies and machines and factories to produce more stuff) -- is driven by and is dependent on the *financial economy*: the invest-earn, buy-sell, spend-earn, *payer-payee money economy*.

The money system -- the monetary system that creates the money supply; and the financial economy within which we use the money to conduct all of our payer-payee money transactions -- is the central nervous system that activates and directs the productive economy.

Money payments are the electrical impulses and the specific information that stimulate workers and businesses to go to work to earn the money that is being spent by the buyers of all the goods, services and assets that are produced by the productive economy and bought-sold for money in the financial economy.

If the financial nervous system fails -- if it stops sending payments signals to the economic body: the economic body just stops working.

It happened in the 1930s. It's happening again now in many countries; because we're still using the same commercial bank-issued zero-sum "repayable bank loan and bond purchase" money supply creation monopoly.

In chapter 4 we'll see how government issuance of debt-free, interest-free money can solve the savings problem: which is debtors' unpayable debts problem, because savers have the same bank deposits that debtors owe back.

And solve the profit problem -- by ongoing injections of new debt-free money into the spend-earn stream, that payees (people and businesses) can earn and accumulate (hold out of circulation): without starving the producer-consumer economy of its circulating money supply; and without increasing debtors' unpayable debts -- which ends in financial crisis and the writeoff of payees' savings.

But before we go there let's have a clear look at the world's biggest secret that is hiding in plain sight.

Money is Numbers

money is numbers

We use money as our numerical payments media: to pay for the stuff we buy and to get paid for the stuff we sell.

"Numerical payments media" means *money is numbers*.

Money is numbers with a $ or £ or € or ¥ sign in front of them.

Money is $numbers that people who sell stuff for money, accept as money payment from people who buy the stuff and pay with money.

Numbers printed on slips of paperlike material are *banknotes*. Numbers stamped on metal discs are *coins*. Numbers in commercial banks deposit accounts are *bank deposits*. Numbers in central bank reserve accounts are *bank reserves*. Numbers in shadow bank cash accounts are *cash balances*.

{And numbers in commercial bank loan accounts and bond accounts are *debts*, which are negative money.}

In each case, the numbers are the money: the amount of money that is owned by the party who has the $1000 of currency in their pocket or the $1000 deposit account balance in their bank account; and the amount of money that is being paid by/paid to when the money is spent-earned.

The numbers indicate "how much money" is being paid by and paid to.

Payees can re-spend the money buying consumer goods, services and assets; and payees can re-invest the money buying producer or investor goods, services and assets.

But the actual thing that is being paid -- transferred from payers to payees -- is the numbers: the numerical amount of money.

And the actual thing that is *owed back* by debtors, is numbers in bank deposit accounts: bank deposits.

[You can't pay your bank loan with the "value" of the surplus supply of food or iPads you produce. First you have to sell the stuff to get paid the buyers' money; then you can pay your debts with the money. During financial crises, producers can't sell the supply of stuff they produce. So indebted businesses -- and their laid-off workers and suppliers -- can't earn enough money to pay their debts.]

The money-value of the money has nothing to do with the economic use value of the materials the numbers are on or in.

Aside from their use as money, the banknotes and coins are economically worthless (except for the small recyclable metal content of the coins).

Most of our money has no physical existence at all. Bank deposits are numbers in bank accounts -- electronic digits in banking system accounting software.

Money is created out of nothing by money-issuers: central banks and commercial banks.

In some nations governments issue the coins. But coins are only about .01% (one ten thousandth) to .1% (one one thousandth) of the total money supply. There are 10s of $billions of coins in circulation so coins are not "nothing".

But compared to the amount of central bank-issued banknotes (3-5% of the money supply); and commercial bank-issued bank deposits (95-97% of the money supply): government-issued coins are a vanishingly small fraction of the total money supply.

[Look at the banknotes in your wallet. Banknotes are not government-issued Treasury Notes like Lincoln's greenbacks. Banknotes are central bank-issued paper money: Federal Reserve Notes (US$ dollars); Bank of Canada Notes (CDN$ dollars); Bank of England Notes (GBR£ pounds); European Central Bank Notes (EUR€ euros); Bank of Japan Notes (JPY¥ yen); Peoples Bank of China Notes (CNY¥ yuan); etc.]

Insofar as the physical cash money is produced: It costs about 17 cents to produce (print) a $20 banknote or a $100 banknote whose money value is 20 dollars or 100 dollars.

It costs almost as much to produce (mint) coins, as the money value of the coins. It costs more than 1 cent to produce a penny, whose money value is 1 cent. It costs about 4 cents to produce a nickel, whose money value is 5 cents.

It costs a few keystrokes for a commercial bank to create a $300,000 bank deposit -- a mortgage loan: a spendable deposit account credit balance in a debtor's bank deposit account.

By typing that number into the Credits column of the debtor's bank deposit account, the bank has created 300 thousand dollars of spendable deposit account credit: a "bank deposit". By typing the negative money version of the same number into the debtor's bank loan account, the bank has created 300 thousand dollars of mortgage loan account *debt*.

The debtor spends the new $300,000 bank deposit -- by certified check or by direct bank account-to-bank account online banking or wire transfer -- by paying the new credit balance to a house seller.

The $300,000 credit balance is debited out of the house buyer's (the mortgage debtor's) bank deposit account balance (which reduces the debtor's spendable bank deposit account balance to $0);

and the payment is credited into the house seller's (the payee's) bank deposit account balance (which increases the payee's spendable bank deposit account balance by +$300,000).

The payee now has the +$300,000 credit balance, which the debtor owes back to the bank as *payment* of the debtor's -$300,000 loan account debt balance.

The debtor earns +$300,000 out of the economy's spend-earn stream, paid into his/her payee bank deposit account by other money-payers (whose deposit account balances are debited to make the payments).

When the debtor earns back the bank deposits and repays the bank loan: the debtor's paid-back deposit account credit balance cancels out the debtor's paid-off loan account debt balance.

The debtor's bank deposit account and bank loan account are restored to their original condition: $0 deposit account credit balance and $0 loan account debt balance.

The deposit account money supply, and debtors' loan account debts, are both cancelled out of existence when debtors repay their bank loans.

"Central bank reserves" are numbers -- reserve account *balances* -- in commercial banks' central bank reserve accounts. The central bank creates reserve account balances by typing numbers --central bank reserves -- into the Credits column of commercial banks' reserve accounts. The credits add to commercial banks' reserve account *balances*.

"Bank deposits" are numbers -- deposit account *balances* -- in customers' commercial bank deposit accounts. Commercial banks create deposit account balances by typing numbers -- bank deposits -- into the Credits column of debtors' bank deposit accounts. The credits add to the debtors' spendable bank deposit account *balances*.

"Cash balances" are numbers -- cash account *balances* -- in customers' shadow bank cash accounts. Cash balances are created when we transfer balances out of our commercial bank deposit accounts, into our shadow bank cash accounts. Our commercial banks debit the transfer amount out of our deposit account balance; and our brokerage credits the transfer amount into our cash account balance. No new money is created when we transfer balances into the "savings-funded" capital markets financial system.

The process by which banks create money is so mind-repellingly simple that when people see it, many people don't believe it.

People keep searching for some "deeper mystery" that makes more sense.

There is no deeper mystery.

Just the tragic reality that the money-using world is held in debt bondage to a global banking cartel that creates the debt-based money supply -- and the unpayable debts -- of people, businesses and nations: by typing numbers into bank accounts.

monetary macroeconomics

Money is numbers that work by arithmetic.

Monetary macroeconomics is money accounting arithmetic: the workings of the monetary system that creates (and un-creates) the money and the credit-debt;

and the workings of the financial economy within which we use the money (currency) and credit-debt (bank deposits) to conduct all of our payer-payee money transactions.

And the effects of changes in the rate of credit-debt expansion (that adds spendable new credit balances into debtors' bank deposit accounts) on the spending-driven producer-consumer economy that is activated and directed by paying and getting paid money: by spending-earning money.

And the primary inflationary-deflationary effects on collateral asset prices (mainly mortgaged real estate) of commercial bank credit-debt expansion (that adds buy-money into mortgage debtors' bank deposit accounts and inflates the sellable price of real estate);

and credit-debt reduction (mortgage debtors try to sell their houses to get money to paydown/payout their mortgage debts, which deflates the sellable price of real estate).

And the secondary inflationary-deflationary effects on financial asset prices in the savings-funded capital markets financial system of commercial bank credit-debt expansion (that adds investible savings into payees' bank deposit accounts, which payees transfer into their shadow bank accounts to invest buying financial assets, which inflates the sellable price of financial assets);

and credit-debt reduction (that extinguishes savings and deflates the sellable price of financial assets).

Money is $numbers that people accept as money payment.

Goods, services and assets are bought-sold for money *prices*; not traded for economic 'values'.

The monetary system that creates the money, and the financial economy within which we use the money, work by arithmetic; not by economic theories.

financial government

The productive economy produces goods, provides services, and builds or makes assets, for sale, for money.

But the productive economy does not produce money.

In order to *have* a a buy-sell for money financial economy: *somebody* has to *create* the money.

Within the present monetary system, that somebody is commercial banks, who create the money supply by making repayable loans of newly-created bank deposits to debtors.

Money creation and allocation constitutes *financial government* of the spending-driven, money-using, money-dependent, buy-sell for money economy.

Everybody needs money.

We do whatever kinds of work somebody will pay us to do; and we produce, provide, build, make, whatever kinds of goods, services and assets somebody will pay to buy from us.

Money commands human action.

We sell our property to get paid the buyer's money. Paying money in a buy-sell, payer-payee transaction *buys ownership* of property.

Creating the buy-money for *somebody* to spend determines *who* will have money to buy ownership of the real economic wealth of nations; and *who*

73

will have money to command human action; and *who* will have money to buy other people's property.

The commercial banking system is the money creation and allocation system that decides who gets how much of the newly created money, for what purposes.

The money power -- the power to create and allocate money; the power to financially govern the money-using world -- has historically been exercised by bankers, not by governments.

Governments issue bond debts to borrow credit that is created by bankers.

In his 1944 book, *The Great Transformation*, Karl Polanyi describes the 19th century process by which Europeans were transformed from citizens of nations under government by God and King; to producers and consumers within market economy under government by the invisible hand of the free market.

Polanyi observed that the invisible hand was attached to the more visible arms and bodies of international bankers who controlled nations' access to credit by controlling the bond market.

Banking families have historically owned the banks; and bankers have historically exercised financial government by controlling money supply creation and allocation via bank loans and bond purchases.

Billions of people and businesses working in the productive economy built up the economic wealth of nations. Read David Korten's 1995 book, *When Corporations Rule the World*, to see who now *owns* most of that wealth.

Privately-owned bank credit-debt creation and allocation is largely responsible for the extremely concentrated *ownership* of the economic wealth and the money; and the widely distributed *debt*.

In his 1936 booklet, *100% Money and the Public Debt*, Irving Fisher wrote, "President John Adams considered any private issue of money a monstrosity and a fraud on the public."

Among the "advantages" Fisher cited in support of his proposed 100% government-issued money system, Fisher included,

"...the Government would recapture its lost franchise and regain its sovereign power over money as granted to it by the Constitution. (and)...the elimination of the management and domination of industry by banks, a common consequence of the freezing of loans during depressions."

But governments have not "recaptured" their lost franchise.

Recapture is probably the wrong term.

Over the 600 year monetary history since the Medici banking family ruled Florence, it has been bankers, not national governments, who issued the money supply of nations;

and who financially governed the debt-issuing, credit-borrowing governments, businesses and people of nations -- by controlling who gets how much of the new credit, for what purposes.

Monetary reformers advocate a *revolutionary change* in "who" issues the money supply of nations; and *who* exercises financial government: bankers? or governments?

"Moderate" monetary reformers advocate *some* government issuance of debt-free money; rather than wholesale conversion from a bank-issued money monopoly to a government-issued money monopoly.

Despite its many and obvious "advantages": converting to a government-issued debt-free money system is easier said than done, as CH Douglas -- author of the "social credit" proposal for a government-issued money system -- discovered when Douglas' social credit ideas gained wide popular support during the 1930s Depression, and presented a real threat to the banks' monopoly of money supply issuance.

Douglas explained "the money problem" -- and his social credit solution -- to the King and government of Norway in a 1935 speech titled, *Money and the Price System* (pdf online),

"It has, as you might say, first the technical side, where you have a system which is operating badly and which under present conditions must continue to operate even worse;

and, secondly, you have an enormous vested interest possessing the most powerful monopoly that the whole history of the world has ever known, the monopoly, as we call it, of credit, the monopoly of the creation of and dealing in money, against which any other monopoly pales into insignificance -- and it is determined to use every weapon to retain this monopoly.

In the modern world it is possible to do without almost any single material thing...but it is practically impossible for any of us to go through twenty-four hours without either money or "credit" which attaches to the belief that we shall have money available sooner or later.

The monopoly of the control of the money system is the great over-riding monopoly of the world as it is worked at the present time.

And, if you just realise -- as you will realise in dealing with this problem -- that it has not merely an economic or mathematical side, but also a side which penetrates into the very highest politics, I will at once leave that political side, to which, however, I merely wanted to refer."

In 1919, while working on an accounting problem for an aircraft manufacturer, Douglas had encountered the profit problem. Businesses add markup to their cost-price of production, in order to sell their outputs at money-profitable above-cost prices.

But businesses paying their costs, becomes consumers' spendable incomes.

Douglas discovered that businesses systematically add more prices into the economy, than they add spendable incomes that can be spent paying those prices.

Douglas' social credit money and price system was his solution to that problem.

But the solution required breaking the banks' monopoly of money supply issuance: converting from a debt-based bank-issued money system to a debt-free government-issued money system.

That's where Douglas encountered the *power* side of the money problem: the power to create and allocate "the money" is the power to financially govern the money-using world.

Like Douglas, I merely wanted to mention the power side of the money problem, before continuing with the easy-to-fix (by issuing debt-free money) arithmetic side of the problem.

Most bankers do not see themselves as part of a financial "government" whose lending decisions determine who gets how much new money, for what purposes; and thereby decide what the money-driven economy will be allowed (and not allowed) to "do".

Most bankers see themselves as financial intermediaries who fund their loans with bank deposits they acquired from their deposit account customers; or who fund their loans with their reserve account balances.

Most bankers try to prudently manage their investment of savers' "loanable funds" by making loans to borrowers who are "credit-worthy": financially able to pay the interest and repay the loan principal out of their earned incomes; or out of the revenues that the borrower will earn by using the bank loan to buy or build income-generating business assets.

Bankers are looking at their individual lending decisions and the financial condition of their individual banks. They are not looking at the monetary system as a whole.

Most bankers assume the monetary *system* "works"; and will continue working in the future as it has worked during the decades since the present credit-debt expansion began in 1939 with bond debt-financed World War 2.

But the commercial banks' repayable bank loan money supply creation monopoly *doesn't* work.

It *can't work*; as a simple matter of arithmetic impossibility.

And when it fails, most commercial bankers are as astonished at their bank's bankruptcy as are their deposit account customers whose deposit account balances get written off.

For an "upside" perspective on the history of banking dating back to the Medicis (and money, dating back to ancient Mesopotamia), read Niall Ferguson's 2008 book, *The Ascent of Money: A Financial History of the World*.

Gold and silver are scarce metal elements; so when gold and silver coins are used as the money supply, money is a scarce commodity. Within a commodity money system, most people don't have any money, or have very little; so most people can't participate in a buy-sell for money economy.

The upside of banking is that the creation of additional bank credit-money enables the development of a financially and economically prosperous buy-sell for money economy.

But banks create credit-money to purchase debtors' debts. If debtors repay their debts (or default on paying their debts), the credit-debt money -- and the financial and economic prosperity -- is extinguished.

Ferguson's book was published in May 2008, 4 months before the September 2008 banking system failure that graphically demonstrated the debtor-default "downside" of commercial banking as the monopoly creator of the world's debt-based money supply.

Even Adam Smith (who, like his contemporaries during the classical era of economic thinking, believed gold is the only "real" money) heaped high praise on the "Scotch banks" whose credit creation increased the amount of money that was circulating in their local economies and enabled a flourishing buy-sell for money economy to develop. {*An Inquiry into the Nature and Causes of the Wealth of Nations*; Book II, Chapter II (1776)}

Smith was aware of the prosperity-generating credit-expansion upside of bank credit-debt creation; but was apparently unaware of the depression-generating debt-reduction downside when debtors have to actually pay back their bank loans and extinguish the credit-debt money supply.

the debt-free money solution

I hope this book's description of the monetary-financial system made it abundantly clear where money does, and does not, come from; and why the commercial banks' credit-debt money supply creation monopoly fails because debtors' debts are unpayable; because payees have all the money; which makes creditors' credits uncollectable; so payees' 'money in the bank' gets written off.

In the next chapter I will present my own version of a "moderate" monetary system reform proposal: an orderly debt reduction program that is enabled by the addition of very significant amounts of debt-free money into the credit-debt money supply.

I am advocating a monetary-fiscal program -- call it a Money Income program -- of adding debt-free money into the deposit account money supply to make the money supply equation positive sum: which enables debtors' loan account debt reduction without an equal reduction of payees' deposit account balances.

Commercial banks' paid-down earning assets (debtors' loan account debt balances) would be replaced with equal new money assets (reserve account balances): to keep banks' balance sheets balanced; and to greatly increase the fraction of fractional reserves the banks hold -- to eliminate the threat of liquidity failure.

The monetary component of the program creates new debt-free money.

The fiscal component of the program pays the new money as a monthly un-earned Money Income into "everybody's" bank deposit accounts.

Debtors' Money Income deposits would be automatically debited to paydown their overdue and underwater loan account debts.

The program requires no changes to any monetary legislation or any of the in-place monetary mechanisms.

After describing the very simple process by which governments and central banks, in conjunction with commercial banks, can create the new debt-free money and pay it into payees' commercial bank deposit accounts;

I will describe the arithmetically predictable effects of adding significant amounts of spendable, investible (and saveable) new money into everybody's commercial bank deposit accounts;

which includes adding significant amounts of debt paydown money into debtors' bank deposit accounts (to solve the savings problem);

and spendable money into consumers' bank deposit accounts (to solve the profit problem).

The Debt-Free Money Income

a money-funded debt reduction program

The Money Income program is a monetary-fiscal debt reduction program.

The program would not be **tax-funded**: the government would not get the money by taking the money from taxpayers.

The program would not be **debt-financed:** the government would not get the money by selling new interest-bearing repayable bond debts to commercial banks and to investors.

The Money Income program would be **money-funded** by the creation of new debt-free, interest-free money in the government's commercial bank deposit accounts, which the government would pay into Money Income recipients' payee bank deposit accounts.

"Everybody" -- every adult citizen -- gets paid the Money Income. This is not a means-tested social welfare program. It's a monetary system debt reduction and solvency restoration program. To be politically fair, you have to pay everybody the same monthly amount.

People who don't owe debts get the Money Income payments too. Those people can spend, invest, or save their Money Income deposits.

Debtors' Money Income deposits will be debited by their banks and extinguished to paydown the debtors' loan account debts.

It is a deficit-spending program.

But instead of *debt-financing* the deficit-spending in the usual way -- by issuing interest-bearing repayable bond debts to borrow newly-created bank deposits from banks and to borrow savings from investors -- the government, central bank, and commercial banks would create new debt-free, interest-free money in the government's commercial bank deposit accounts to *money-fund* the government's Money Income payments.

zero interest perpetual bonds

Government bond debts are term loans. Until the term expires, the government doesn't pay any of the loan principal, only the interest. The Treasury debts all have a maturity date. When the term expires and the debt matures, the "loan principal" comes due for repayment.

Then the government has to collect taxes from its citizens and businesses; or sell new bonds to banks and investors; to get money to pay to the banks and investors (bond-holders) who own the government's due-for-payment bond debts.

Perpetual bonds have no maturity date. Adair Turner describes how the British government used to issue "consols" -- interest-bearing perpetual bonds with no maturity date. The government would pay its semi-annual bond interest to the bond-holders; but the bonds *never* came due for repayment.

The government *could* collect taxes and pay back the money to buy back (redeem; extinguish) the perpetual bonds, if it chose to do so.

"Redemption" of perpetual bonds -- repaying the money to buy back the bonds from the bond-holders -- is the choice of the bond-*issuer* (the debtor); not the bond-*holder* (the creditor).

So the consol-issuing British government never had to repay the loans. The government only had to pay the twice-yearly interest payments on the perpetual loans.

Lincoln's government money-funded some of its deficit-spending by printing debt-free, interest-free paper cash money and spending the paper money paying the soldiers and suppliers who contributed to the North's Civil War effort.

Within the modern electronic monetary system: government issuance of *zero-interest* perpetual bonds can create effectively debt-free and interest-free new electronic bank account money -- bank deposits -- to money-fund the Money Income program.

creating debt-free bank account money (bank deposits) within the present central-commercial banking system

The government would issue zero interest perpetual bonds and sell them to commercial banks, who pay for their asset purchases in the usual way: by typing spendable credits -- bank deposits -- into the bond-selling government's commercial bank deposit accounts.

The commercial banks then sell the perpetual bonds to the central bank, who pays for its asset purchases in the usual way: by typing credits -- central bank reserves -- into the bond-selling commercial banks' central bank reserve accounts.

That's it.

That is the monetary part of the program: creating new debt-free, interest-free bank deposits: spendable $numbers in the government's commercial bank deposit accounts; electronic payments money.

And creating equal new reserve account balances in commercial banks' reserve accounts, when commercial banks sell the government's new perpetual debts to the central bank.

The government now has debt-free, interest-free, fully reserve-backed, spendable bank deposits in its commercial bank deposit accounts.

The fiscal part of the Money Income program is the government paying the new bank deposits into citizens' payee bank deposit accounts, as a monthly un-earned Money Income.

The government either transfers the new bank deposits into its central bank account and pays the Money Income payments out of its central bank account; or the government pays the new bank deposits directly out of its commercial bank deposit accounts into payees' commercial bank deposit accounts; both ways via the normal debiting/crediting operation of the payments system.

The government authorizes the electronic payments to the Money Income payees; the banks debit payer (government) deposit account balances and credit payee (citizens) deposit account balances.

That's it.

That is the fiscal part of the program: getting the new debt-free money to where it is needed.

New debt-free, interest-free, 100% reserve-backed bank deposits have been created and paid into citizens' bank deposit accounts as an un-earned Money Income.

At no present or future cost to anybody.

Banks then debit their loan account customers' Money Income deposits and credit that amount as a payment against the debtors' loan account debts.

The debtors' new Money Income deposit account balances, and an equal amount of the debtors' old loan account debt balances, are extinguished out of existence.

That is all that is needed to accomplish the objective of the program: debtors' loan account debt reduction without equally reducing the deposit account balances of the people and businesses who earned and now own the present deposit account money supply.

By enabling paydown of otherwise unpayable individual and household debts (which restores solvency to individuals and households); the Money Income program reduces distressed (defaulting) debt-assets and increases reserves (money assets) on commercial banks' balance sheets, which restores solvency to banks.

Payees (recipients of the Money Income) who don't owe debts could save, spend or invest their Money Incomes.

The primary purpose of the Money Income program is to restore solvency to deeply-indebted debtor-individuals and households and their equally at-risk creditor-banks by a program of orderly debt paydown.

Heavily-indebted Money Income recipients -- even if they are current on their loan payments -- could use their Money Income deposits to voluntarily accelerate paydown of their underwater mortgages, home equity loans, student loans, car loans, credit card debts, line of credit and overdraft debts, etc.

The zero interest perpetual bonds would not be "marketable" securities: they would not be held by commercial banks or sold into the capital markets.

Governments would issue them, commercial banks would create new bank deposits to buy them from the government, and central banks would create new reserve account balances in commercial banks' reserve accounts to buy the perpetual bonds from commercial banks.

The central bank would hold the perpetual bonds on its own central bank balance sheet "in perpetuity".

Bond debts that never have to be repaid are not "real" debts.

Zero interest perpetual bonds have no interest cost to the bond-issuer, ever.

And because the new bank deposits *never* have to be paid back to redeem the government's perpetual bonds, this program adds a permanent supply of debt-free, interest-free bank deposits into the deposit account money supply.

Which transforms the deposit account money supply from a zero sum equation to a positive sum equation. The kind of money supply that can be "saved" without crashing the banking system.

QE for the economy

The money-funded Money Income is an orderly credit-debt reduction program to *prevent* the banking system failure, credit-debt writedowns, and Debt-Deflation Depression that is otherwise arithmetically inevitable.

The program is QE for the economy. "Helicopter money", dropped into household bank accounts to enable orderly debt paydown. Steve Keen calls it a modern day Debt Jubilee; a cleaning of the slates.

Except in this kind of slate-cleaning, creditors get all their money back, rather than losing it to systemic debtor defaults and credit-debt writedowns.

Mass debtor default is the business-as-usual way of cleaning the slates -- the banks' balance sheets -- of all the uncollectable credits and unpayable debts and bankrupt banks at the end of a credit-debt expansion supercycle.

The Money Income program accomplishes the same credit-debt writedowns, without taking the banking system -- and people's and businesses' already existing deposit account money supply -- down with it.

QE for banks has been and is adding liquidity (bank reserves) into commercial banks' reserve accounts.

Central banks have taken the necessary actions to prevent banking system liquidity failure. QE enables debtor-banks to pay their deposit liability debts owed to their creditor-depositors.

QE for the economy adds liquidity (bank deposits) into debtor-households' bank deposit accounts.

The Money Income deposits paid into payees' bank accounts enables debtor households to pay their loan account debts owed to their creditor-banks...

and owed to capital markets investors who bought the securitized debts (MBS; CDOs) to hold as interest-earning assets in their brokerage accounts.

how much should the Money Income be?

As a monetary system salvation program, the Money Income payments should be enough to enable rapid restoration of solvency to debtor-households and their creditor-banks.

The Money Income deposits should be enough to enable debtors to make their loan payments, but not so much that they discourage people from seeking paid work.

Paying the Money Income in relatively small monthly payments would be least disruptive to the banking and financial system. Most household debts are payable monthly, so monthly Money Income payments match debtors' debt payment obligations.

The initial monthly amount does not have to be permanent. The program can be adjusted, or discontinued, once solvency is restored.

I suggest $1000 per month, using the US$ system as an example.

If the Money Income in the US was $1000 per month per citizen 18 and over with a Social Security number, then a 2 adult household would receive $2000 per month of this un-earned Income.

$1000 per month individual Money Income is enough to make student loans and car loans and credit card payments payable.

$2000 per month household Money Income, added to households' present earned incomes, is enough to make most household debts -- including mortgage and home equity loan debts and line of credit and overdraft debts -- payable.

The Money Income would be electronically credited into "everybody's" commercial bank deposit accounts via the bank-operated payments system, so the banks would simply debit their debtors' $1000 Money Income deposits and credit $1000 against the debtors' overdue mortgage or other loan payments.

In the case of 2 adult households, they would have $2000 per month of Money Income to apply against their mortgage and other loan payments.

About 1/3 of all student loans are presently "delinquent": the loan payments are not being made because the student debtors "have no money".

Students would have $1000 per month Money Income to pay their student loan debts; and banks would have $1000 per month Money Income deposits to collect their interest-earning assets, to bring the delinquent loan payments up to date.

A large percentage of car loan debts, and credit card debts, is also delinquent. Individuals and households could make their credit card and car loan payments; and pay down their lines of credit and overdrafts.

A $1000 per month Money Income program would rapidly restore most individual and household loans to "current" status.

And as total loans are paid down, banks' interest-earning debt-assets are reduced down to the realistically sellable price of banks' collateral assets: heavily mortgaged real estate, mainly {and "distressed" government bond debts in the eurozone}.

Bank solvency is restored by paying down banks' defaulting debt-assets and increasing their non-defaultable money-assets -- their reserve account balances.

Banks' total deposit liabilities are not reduced, because debtors' debts are paid down with the new Money Income deposits, rather than paid down with deposit account customers' previously existing deposit account balances. Commercial banks' balance sheets would actually be expanded, with additional new deposit liabilities and equal new reserve assets.

By solidifying the asset side of bank balance sheets -- by replacing defaulting debt-assets with non-defaultable money-assets (reserves); the deposit liability side is solidified.

In this sense the Money Income functions as a monetary system SOS program.

You bail out the credit-issuing banks and the credit-using economy, by bailing out the banks' defaulting debtors.

You reduce debtors' total loan account debts, without reducing payees' total deposit account money supply.

So in the first place, the Money Income program rapidly deleverages both debtor-households and creditor-banks, to restore financial solvency and stability.

And the 100% reserve-backing of the new Money Income deposit account balances (many of which are extinguished paying down debtors' loan account debts) secures an equal amount of deposit account customers' already existing deposit account balances with the 100% central bank money-backing of *all* the new Money Income deposit account balances, including those that are extinguished in debtors' loan account debt paydowns.

The program adds more net new reserves into commercial banks' reserve accounts, than it adds net new bank deposits into customers' bank deposit accounts.

The "fraction" of bank reserves (money assets) to bank deposit liabilities (money liabilities) is increased; and the fraction of (uncollectable) earning assets to bank deposit liabilities is reduced.

Banks would have a bigger fraction of non-defaultable money assets -- rather than defaultable debt-assets -- to back their money liabilities.

And the bigger fraction of reserves would be permanent, because the central bank would never sell the government's zero interest perpetual bonds to commercial banks in open market operations, and commercial banks would never pay reserves to buy the bonds and hold them on their own balance sheets.

The central bank's balance sheet is *permanently expanded* with new perpetual reserve liabilities (commercial banks' permanently bigger reserve account balances) and new perpetual debt-assets (the government's new non-repayable, zero interest perpetual bond debts).

[Japan is already more or less doing this, without saying it is doing it. New Japanese government bonds are sold to Japanese commercial banks who create new yen bank deposits to buy them; then the central Bank of Japan almost immediately buys the government's debts from the commercial banks (and pays by creating more excess reserves in the commercial banks' reserve accounts) and holds the bonds on its own balance sheet. The government deficit-spends the new commercial bank-issued bank deposits into Japan's spend-earn money stream, which keeps the stream liquid with new money-spending; which enables money-earners to accumulate yen bank deposits as savings without starving the economy of its circulating money supply.]

where would the new money go?

On a very rough estimate (and because the totals divide nicely into thirds), about 225 million US citizens would qualify -- age 18 and older with a Social Security number -- for the Money Income.

At $1000 per month per citizen times 12 months, that sums up to $2.7 trillion per year of newly issued debt-free money added directly into the US economy's deposit account money supply.

Recipients must first use their Money Income deposits for overdue debt paydowns. We do not have administrative access to our bank accounts: we cannot debit and credit our own bank accounts. Overdue debtors would never have access to their Money Income deposits. They would be paid a credit, which their bank would debit to make the debtor's overdue loan payments.

But people who are current on their debts, or who are debt-free, simply receive $12,000 per year of additional income to spend, save or invest as they please.

Or to accelerate paydown of their underwater mortgages, which benefits both the underwater debtors and their technically insolvent banks who are holding those balance sheet debt-assets and collateral assets at still-inflated valuations.

I am guessing that about 1/3 of all Money Income payments -- at least over the first 3-4 years of the program -- would go directly toward paying down mortgages and paying down the overdue and otherwise unpayable debts of heavily indebted individuals and households. This portion of the new money is simply "extinguished", along with the debt that it extinguishes.

+$1000 of new deposit account money paid against -$1000 of old loan account debt = $0 new money and $0 old debt in the debtor's bank deposit and bank loan accounts. The new money is extinguished to paydown the old debts.

[Banks might complain that their interest-earning debt-assets are being paid down by "government policy". But if the banks need interest income, the central bank can pay interest on the banks' permanently increased new reserve account balances.

If the alternative to paying down banks' *uncollectable* interest-earning debt-assets to solvent levels is regulatory enforcement of business accounting standards -- which would involve "recognition" of banks' uncollectable earning assets (loan losses and bank bankruptcies) -- banks aren't really in a position to dictate terms of their salvation.]

Money that is extinguished in bank loan repayments no longer "exists".

So 1/3 of the Money Income deposits cannot contribute to any kind of spending-driven price inflation; because 1/3 of the new money will be extinguished to paydown debtors' debts.

The program merely leaves an equal amount of payees' already existing deposit account balances intact -- now fully backed with central bank reserves -- while paying down large amounts of debtors' otherwise unpayable loan account debts.

Another 1/3 of the Money Income payments would go to households who are presently able to afford their loan payments out of their earned incomes and capital incomes, but who would be far more comfortable and secure with less debt. So I'm guessing this group would use 1/2 of their Money Income to reduce their debts; and save, spend and invest the other half in about equal amounts.

[Only about .01% of the population is "rich" in monthly earned incomes, in money savings, and in capital income-generating financial assets. Almost everybody depends on their monthly earned incomes -- not their savings or capital incomes -- to get money to pay their monthly cost of living spending and loan payments; and to add to their savings and investible capital. Almost everybody would "feel" the financial effects of being paid $1000 per month of un-earned Money Income.]

The final 1/3 of the Money Income payments would go to households who are already fairly financially sound, who owe little or no debt, and who earn sufficient incomes to pay for the cost of living they already enjoy.

This group would tend to save and invest their Money Income deposits.

Which adds to the global savings glut and the glut of investible capital.

Which further inflates the buy-sell prices -- and depresses the yields -- of investment assets like stocks, bonds and rental real estate.

But at least ongoing demand to buy investment assets would prevent asset prices from deflating and wiping out $trillions of "paper wealth".

Paper wealth is better than paper poverty.

And in huge liquid markets, many individual investors can cash out without crashing the price of the investments they are selling. Financial markets "work" when they have enough money flowing into them from investment buyers, to enable money flowing out of them to investment sellers.

And what will cashers-out do with the money?

Cashers-out can save the money in physical cash or in bank/brokerage account money-balances that pay zero or near-zero interest.

The Money Income program *prevents* the mass debtor defaults and Debt-Deflation Depression that deflates the sellable price of assets. So there is no benefit to sitting on deposit balances and cash balances waiting for asset prices to deflate so you can buy them up at debt-distressed liquidation sale prices.

Or cashers-out can spend (invest) the money paying the capital costs of building new productive infrastructure to produce new economic wealth -- assets, goods, services -- for sale.

Investing the capital cost money into the "real" economy adds money-incomes -- which become consumer-incomes -- to all the businesses, workers and suppliers who are being paid to actually build the new productive capacity.

Adding spendable consumer earned incomes enables the investors to sell the new stuff they will produce. Adding additional un-earned Money

Incomes enables more consumer spending and producer earning; at money-profitable prices.

Or cashers-out can spend the money on consumption. The spending of large concentrations of money savings on the building of mansions and yachts is a private version of Keynesian fiscal stimulus that distributes the previously saved money to hundreds of businesses, workers and suppliers who are paid to build the consumer luxuries.

Or cashers-out can use the money to bid up the buy-sell price of the world's very limited supply of money metals like gold and silver, to hold as their end-of-the-capitalist-world Doomsday personal money supply.

Investment-spending puts the economy to work building capital assets and consumer assets and producing goods and services. The businesses and workers who provide the inputs and do the work earn the money that is being spent by the investors.

Buying money metals at inflated prices -- as an end-of-the-world insurance policy -- enriches the sellers of the money metals. Now the metal-sellers have to "do something" with the money; just like capital markets sellers of price-inflated stocks and bonds have to do something with the money.

Saving the money simply holds it out of circulation, and generates no financial or economic activity and no returns to savers.

The buy-sell prices of stuff can only be inflated if the money is *spent* buying the stuff. Saving money only inflates numbers in bank accounts. Bank deposits will continue to pay zero or slightly negative interest. If your money is not *doing* anything, how is it going to "increase"?

[Banks don't pay interest to attract deposits because they need the deposits to fund their loans. Every bank loan and bond purchase is funded with the bank's creation of a brand new bank deposit in the debtor's bank deposit account.

For an "interesting" take on interest, read Steve Randy Waldman's Interfluidity blog post, *the negative un-natural rate of interest* (published in 2011; available online) in which Waldman suggests that savers should *pay* to have somebody else carry their financial wealth forward into the future for them.

Instead of being paid interest on idle savings account balances, customers would pay (small) monthly service fees to banks for holding their money.

If everybody is also being paid a monthly un-earned Money Income that is a lot bigger than almost everybody's monthly interest income from their savings account balances, then paying banks to securely hold your money might seem a little less "un-natural".]

savings and securitization

Capital markets "securitization" -- commercial banks originate bank loans, then sell the interest-earning debt-assets to investment banks, who bundle the debts into "securities" (like MBS and CDOs) and sell the interest-earning securities to capital markets investors who have transferred their commercial bank account savings into their shadow bank cash accounts -- uses (in a roundabout manner) savers' savings to fund bank loans; rather than using newly-created bank deposits to fund the loans.

Which is a more complicated version of what virtually every monetary system *reformer* advocates: converting commercial banks from deposit-*creating* monetary institutions to deposit-*taking* financial intermediaries who get loanable funds from their depositors then lend out and invest their depositors' savings, and share the interest-earnings with the savers who provide the "funding" for the bank loans.

Since Glass-Steagall was repealed, many commercial banks already own (or are co-owned or partnered with) investment banks and brokerages. Commercial banks already offer savers the opportunity to invest their savings by transferring balances into their brokerage accounts and investing their cash balances buying interest-earning debt-assets like government bonds, and private sector MBS and CDOs.

Adding a monthly Money Income payment into everybody's (including debtors') bank deposit accounts enables the debtors -- whose mortgages and car loans are the "interest-earning assets" that are bundled into the MBS and CDOs -- to *pay* their loan principal and interest payments.

Which enables investors in MBS and CDOs to *earn* the interest payments by lending (via their banks/brokers) their savings to the debtors.

Securitization is a good system; a good way of re-circulating some of the global 10s of $trillions of non-circulating savings account balances. And the system -- the commercial bank loan origination system; and the shadow bank securitization system; is already in place.

Adding a monthly Money Income payment into everybody's commercial bank deposit account makes savers' investment of their savings in MBS and CDOs "secure": because the debtors' Money Income deposits would be debited to make the debtors' loan principal and interest payments.

Debtors would have a secure source of Money Income to *pay* their interest-bearing debts, and for creditors to *collect* their interest-earning assets.

And securitization offers savers an alternative to negative interest rates (paying monthly service fees, instead of getting paid monthly interest) on their otherwise idle savings account balances.

Commercial banks would no longer pay interest on their customers' savings account balances to try to attract savers' transfers of bank deposits from other banks, because the Money Income program adds very large amounts of reserves into commercial banks' reserve accounts, so commercial banks would not need to attract deposits in order to get the reserves (reserve account settlements) that follow the bank deposits.

So negative interest rates on idle savings account balances would probably become a permanent feature of a "reformed" monetary system that adds debt-free money into the deposit account money supply; and adds equal new reserves into commercial banks' reserve accounts.

[Some currency systems are experimenting with negative yields on bank deposits. Instead of getting paid interest on your deposit account balance, you pay your bank monthly service fees.

As an attempt to discourage saving and encourage spending*, this is a failure. People save even more of their earned incomes, to make up for the money they lose on their negative-yield bank deposit account balances. Saving is a very deep-seated human desire.

Which is why we need a positive sum money supply system that can accommodate saving without crashing the (zero-sum credit-debt) monetary system and writing off the savings.

*Negative yield bank deposits is somewhat similar to Silvio Gesell's early-20th century idea of "stamp money"; which was actually implemented in the Austrian town of Worgl in 1932-33. The local government issued paper scrip money to the townspeople, which the people used to pay each other. Which revived the Depression-era town's buy-sell, spend-earn economy by providing the people with some "money" to spend-earn.

Every month the people had to have the money stamped, and pay a price of 1% of the value of the money for the stamp. Which encouraged people to re-spend the scrip, rather than have to pay 1% per month to hold it out of circulation from the town's spend-earn money stream.]

So even though savings account balances will continue to pay slightly negative, zero, or near-zero interest: much of the new Money Income deposits would probably just be saved in now safe -- because more heavily reserve-backed -- bank accounts.

Bank service fees on savings accounts would be small, which means the "negative interest rate" would be very small, so the cost of safely storing your financial wealth in savings accounts would be very small.

Even if you don't actually *do* anything with the money, ever, it's still nice to "look at" a nice fat balance at the bottom of your bank deposit account statement.

There is personal "value" in the simple security of "having money"...and knowing it's there to spend if you need it; and not at risk of writeoff by bank bankruptcy or depositor bail-in.

Money-earners "hoard the money".

Which is why a repayable bank loan money supply creation monopoly doesn't work.

We're not going to change human nature.

Adding debt-free Money Income deposits into the credit-debt money supply accommodates people's desire to "have money", permanently, without crashing the banks' repayable bank loan money supply creation system and writing off the savings.

how fast would debts be paid down?

By my (admittedly very rough) estimates, about 1/2 of all Money Income deposits would simply be extinguished in debt paydowns.

So if the total payment of Money Incomes to US adult citizens is $2.7 trillion per year, $1.35 trillion would be extinguished paying down $1.35 trillion per year of loan account debt.

Over a period of years, overleveraged creditor-banks and overindebted debtor-households would deleverage down to stable and affordable levels.

A 2 adult household that receives $24,000 per year in Money Income deposits could paydown $120,000 of their mortgage and other debts over 5 years, for example.

Many households finance their small business investments with personal debt, so small business debts would also be reduced by this program.

According to the Federal Reserve Board of Governors Financial Accounts of the United States for the First Quarter 2017: total US household debt as of March 31, 2017 was $14.9 trillion.

Total household mortgage debt is $9.836 trillion.

Many of those mortgages are still underwater: the debtor owes more money against the house, than the sellable price of the house.

Millions of people are still struggling to make monthly mortgage payments on the inflated prices they paid for houses during the 2000s real estate price bubble.

Many of those mortgage loans are delinquent (debtors are not making the loan payments). Many are still in the process of defaulting.

The average US household with debt is carrying about $16,000 of credit card debt and owes total debt of over $140,000.

Heavily-indebted households owe much higher than the "average" debt.

And many people are rolling over their total debt -- juggling new loans from different lenders to make loan payments to other lenders -- rather than paying down their total debts.

And since 2010, total credit-debt is increasing again, which increases total unpayable debt because the payees -- people, businesses, corporations -- who earn the debtors' new spending are saving some of their earnings rather than re-spending or re-investing them all.

Most of the new bank deposits are flowing into the bank accounts and brokerage accounts of the top few percentiles of money-earners. Which will end in mass debtor-defaults and the next banking system Collapse.

Total student loan debt is $1.438 trillion, and about 1/3 of student loans are presently "delinquent": the student-debtor has no job, no income (or a low paid job that barely pays the debtor's minimal monthly cost of living spending), and is not making the loan payments.

Total car loan debt is $1.2 trillion, and a significant percentage of those loans are also delinquent.

It is the unpayable debts of these individuals and households that are the target of this Money Income debt reduction program. These debtors and their creditor-banks are the banking system "debtor default and bank bankruptcy" threat that the Money Income program prevents.

Paying "everybody" the same $1000 per month Money Income addresses the political issue of "fairness". Everybody's financial position rises by the same $1000 per month.

If you already have money and don't owe debts, you will have more money. Deeply below $0 debtors and their creditor-banks simply rise up from deep negative depths closer toward daylight at $0.

I picked $1000 per month per adult citizen as the Money Income amount because it is large enough to be visibly effective, but not too large or too fast to be too disruptive.

Governments could set up automatic debits to pay the Money Income deposits into payees' bank deposit accounts. Debtors and their creditor-banks could set up automatic debits to paydown debtors' loan account debts.

The credits and debits would be performed by computers running banking system accounting software. It would not require 1000s of new bank employees typing on keyboards.

But commercial banks would have to be paid service fees for their participation in administering this debt reduction program.

That could be accomplished by selling the government's perpetual bonds to commercial banks at a slight discount from their face value; then the central bank would buy the bonds from commercial banks at face value; so commercial banks earn the price increase as their business income -- their "service fee" for participating in the program.

would the Money Income cause price inflation?

There are 2 different kinds of prices that can inflate (and deflate): asset prices and consumer goods and services prices (CPI prices).

About half of the Money Income deposits -- $1.35 trillion per year -- would be extinguished in bank loan paydowns.

That leaves about $1.35 trillion of spendable, investible, and saveable money injected per year by this program. Which is a significant, but by no means excessive, fiscal stimulus. And it's not targeted at people who would spend the money.

Many people would probably leave most or all of their Money Income in their now-safe bank savings accounts, to add to their emergency funds, retirement savings, and the simple financial security of having money in the bank.

Money saved in bank accounts does not "fund" anything. Nobody is lending, spending or investing those savings, so adding savings to bank accounts cannot cause any CPI or asset price inflation. I'll guess that 1/3 of the $1.35 trillion -- $450 billion per year -- would be saved in bank accounts.

The additional deposit liabilities on commercial banks' balance sheets are matched dollar for dollar by the additional reserves (money assets) the central bank issues to buy the government's zero interest perpetual bonds from the commercial banks. And the new reserve account balances are permanent new money assets held against the banks' new deposit liabilities.

Essentially, the Money Income deposits become Irving Fisher's 100% reserve-backed money.

Total debt-backed deposit account *credit* is reduced.

Total reserve-backed deposit account *money* is increased.

We would actually have more 100% reserve-backed "money" in our bank deposit accounts.

As Fisher pointed out in 1936, there would be no need for deposit insurance because there would be no reason for runs on banks. So that would save banks the cost of paying for deposit insurance.

Another 1/3 of the $1.35 trillion would probably be spent, which adds $450 billion per year of consumer spending into the US economy's $18.57 trillion (2016) GDP. Which is a 2.4% increase in total spending.

In a fully employed economy, adding 2.4% more money-spending might cause some CPI inflation. But in an economy with a lot of unemployed and underemployed workers and idle productive capacity, the spending would increase producers' sales volumes and sales revenues; which motivates an increase of production of goods and services for sale and employment of workers, rather than inflating the sellable price of the existing volume of production of consumer goods and services.

Insofar as CPI prices are inflated, *everybody* is being paid $12,000 per year of un-earned Money Income. Which more than compensates for any loss of purchasing power of most people's present money savings.

Most people do not *have* any significant amount of savings.

69% of Americans have less than $1000 of savings.

34% of Americans have $0 savings.

An additional 35% have $1 - $999 savings.

11% have $1000 - $4,999 savings.

5% have $5,000 - $9,999 savings.

Only 15% of Americans have $10,000 or more of 'money in the bank'.

$10,000 of savings is enough to pay a household's basic cost of living spending (food, utilities, rent or mortgage payment; car or transportation costs); and other monthly debt payments (for clothes, electronics, home furnishings, etc, that were paid for with credit card debt or line of credit/overdraft debt): for about 4 months.

People depend on their earned incomes to get money to buy food and pay their bills. People depend on "having incomes", not on "having savings". Most people have far less than $10,000 of savings. Many people are 1 or 2 paychecks away from debt default and bankruptcy.

And you don't earn interest and gain purchasing power on your "net worth". Owning a mortgage-free house that is "worth" $500,000 does not earn you any interest. You earn interest on your "money"; not on your "wealth".

You earn interest on your commercial bank savings account balances; and you earn interest on your CDs (certificates of deposit). You earn interest on your loaned-out brokerage account cash balance (your money market funds); and you earn interest on your brokerage account holdings of government and corporate bond debts and securitized consumer debts.

Most "wealthy" people do not own a lot of "liquid money": commercial bank checking account balances and savings account balances; and shadow bank cash account balances. Most wealthy people own mortgage-free and debt-free personal assets (houses, cars, etc); and own income-generating investment assets like businesses, stocks, bonds and rental real estate.

Most wealthy people have much less than $1 million of money savings.

If you have $1.2 million of money savings in your bank accounts; and if the Money Income program adds 1% to CPI inflation; then your money savings lose $12,000 per year of purchasing power; but you get $12,000 per year of Money Income deposits to add to your money savings; so you break even in terms of purchasing power.

Everyone who has less than $1.2 million of money savings gains more purchasing power than they lose. Everyone who has more than $1.2 million of money savings loses more purchasing power than they gain.

Loss of purchasing power due to money supply expansion acts as a "tax" on large holdings of money savings: devalues the purchasing power of the existing money supply. This cannot be avoided.

It already happens when debtors and their creditor-banks expand the deposit account money supply, which, as we saw earlier, directly inflates the buy-sell price of mortgageable assets (especially real estate); and indirectly inflates the buy-sell price of financial assets (stocks and bonds); and indirectly inflates the buy-sell price of consumer goods and services (CPI prices).

But within the commercial banks' money supply issuance *monopoly*, nobody is "compensating" savers by adding an un-earned Money Income into their deposit account balances; an income that is money-funded, so it doesn't cost present or future taxpayers any of their money.

And the alternative to the Money Income program is not maintaining the present purchasing power of your savings. The alternative is bailing-in and writing off some of your savings to forestall the bank bankruptcies that would entirely extinguish your savings.

Forestalling means putting off, not preventing.

The money-funded Money Income program can permanently prevent the bail-ins and bank bankruptcies, by paying down debtors' unpayable debts that are owed to already insolvent creditor-banks who are "insolvent" because they can't *collect* their earning assets -- the debtors' defaulting mortgage loans, student loans, car loans, credit card loans, line of credit and overdraft loans, small business loans, etc.

The zero-sum bank loan money supply creation monopoly *doesn't work.*

Zero-sum credit-debt needs a positive sum money supplement, to make it work. Both financial systems -- the commercial banking system and the capital markets financial system -- need a stable base of money.

The money-funded Money Income program -- which adds new bank reserves equally as it adds new bank deposits -- provides that stable base of "100% Money".

Most of the Money Income that is spent, would be spent paying local landlords, retailers and service providers -- which was Milton Friedman's rationale for his negative income tax (1962) and his automatic transfer payments (1948).

Friedman understood that in a buy-sell for money producer-consumer economy, money flows "up".

By adding a stable base of spendable consumer incomes at the bottom, you add a stable base of demand-spending that businesses can earn as their rents, sales revenues, and service fees. Which supports a stable base of business investment in production of stuff for sale, and worker/supplier employment and consumer incomes earned by contributing to the production of that stuff.

Because the US imports a significant portion of its consumer goods, foreign producers (and their workers/suppliers) would end up earning some of the annual $450 billion of added US consumer spending. In a globalized economy with free trade, this kind of "leakage" cannot be avoided.

[And virtually every nation on Earth is presently suffering the same credit-debt financial crisis. So if some "big" money systems (like the US$, European euro, British pound, Japanese yen, Chinese yuan) did it, this debt-free money-funded Money Income program would likely be replicated by every currency system. Ideally it could be coordinated globally so that each nation adds proportionate amounts to its money supply, so current fx valuations would not be affected by some nations adding to their total money supply (and paying down their domestic debts) while others are not.]

The final 1/3 of the $1.35 trillion would probably be transferred from bank accounts to brokerage accounts to be invested, which would add $450 billion per year to the glut of investible savings that is presently maintaining asset prices at historic heights.

Adding even more investible funds -- $450 billion per year -- would prevent what many value investors expect to be the 'inevitable' deep downward 'correction' of presently sky-high asset prices as the market "returns to normal".

We do not want to return "to normal". Normal is the credit-debt supercycle of credit expansion prosperity followed by financial collapse and debt-deflation depression with mass bankruptcies and $trillions of saver and investor money and asset losses.

This debt-free money injection program is designed to *prevent* the financial collapse and debt-deflation depression part of the cycle.

Asset prices will remain inflated. Yields will remain depressed. It will be harder to earn more money just by owning assets.

But investors will be compensated for ongoing low investment returns by their annual receipt of $12,000 of un-earned Money Income payments. The Money Income would be tax-free.

$12,000 per year of tax-free Money Income is the equivalent of earning 3% per year after-tax net on $400,000 of invested household savings.

A 2 adult household would receive $24,000 per year of tax-free Money Income, which is the equivalent of earning 6% after tax net on $400,000 of invested household savings.

Which is better than losing your invested money entirely in a financial collapse and deflationary depression that bankrupts many of the bond-debtors and businesses whose bonds and stocks investors own as our "investment assets".

Solvency is a liberating experience. As is the financial security of having secure bank account savings that you can spend if you have to; and secure capital markets investments that pay at least *some* capital income and that you can sell to get money if you have to.

the Money Income program does not replace existing monetary and fiscal programs

The Money Income program does not *replace* any other current government program spending. It could do that in the future, after solvency is restored to the overleveraged banking system and the over-indebted credit-using economy -- which, at $1000 per month, would take a few years.

For example, insofar as most social welfare programs are income supplement programs -- giving money to poor people so they can buy what they need from "the economy" -- a Money Income could replace most of those welfare programs.

This was Milton Friedman's rationale for a (tax-funded) negative income tax (presented in his 1962 book, *Capitalism and Freedom*); and his earlier idea of a money-funded system of automatic transfer payments (presented in his 1948 policy paper, *A Monetary and Fiscal Framework for Economic Stability*).

Friedman -- like all financially literate monetary macroeconomists -- understood that money flows up as goods and services flow down. Poor people tend to spend most of the money they receive, paying their very modest cost of living spending.

By "putting a floor under personal incomes", Friedman's automatic income-supplement programs would provide a stable base of rental income for landlords and a stable base of sales revenues and service fees for local businesses who provide the goods and services that poor people buy with their incomes.

Poor people get the housing, goods, and services that they need. Landlords and businesses get the money. Consumers get richer in goods. Producers get richer in money.

So in due course, a (possibly) more limited version of the money-funded Money Income program could replace existing tax-funded income-supplement social welfare programs.

But right now we're not trying to "improve" an already well-functioning monetary (money supply-creating) and financial (money-using) system. We're trying to prevent monetary-cum-financial-cum-economic Collapse.

The zero interest perpetual bond-based money-funding of the Money Income program does not replace governments' current bond debt financing of their deficit spending.

Interest-bearing Treasury debt is the "risk free asset" that provides the stable base upon which commercial banks and shadow banks have constructed gargantuan inverted pyramids of credit-debt.

The monetary component of the Money Income program stabilizes commercial bank balance sheets by replacing risk assets (defaulting debts) with money assets (reserves). To stabilize the heavily-leveraged capital markets financial system requires more "risk-free" collateral, which is more "government debt".

Within the present monetary system, primary dealer commercial banks issue new bank deposits to purchase new issues of Treasury debt, then the commercial banks sell some of the Treasury debts to the central bank who issues new reserves to purchase the debt-assets.

Selling new bonds to commercial banks in the primary dealer system is how governments "get" deficit-spending money (bank deposits).

Selling the debt-assets to the central bank in the secondary markets is how commercial banks "get reserves" in their reserve accounts (base money; money assets; liquidity).

Commercial banks selling Treasury debt to shadow banks in the secondary markets is how the shadow banking system acquires its "risk-free collateral assets".

The existing supply of government bond debt matures. The mature bills, notes and bonds are paid out and extinguished. The existing supply of risk-free banking system assets has to be rolled over.

Which means primary dealer banks need to be able to buy new issues of interest-bearing Treasury debt, which they can sell to shadow banks in the secondary (capital) markets.

And central banks need to be able to buy and sell interest-bearing Treasury debt in open market operations, to perform their interest rate-influencing monetary policy operations.

Which means governments still need to debt-finance their deficit spending by issuing new interest-bearing bond debts, which commercial banks can buy from the government then sell to the central bank and to shadow banks to provide a stable base of risk-free collateral assets to the shadow banking system.

Eventually we may be able to transform from a debt-based money system to more of a money-based banking system. The 100% reserve-backed bank deposits that money-fund the Money Income program move the system in that direction.

But right now, starving commercial and shadow banks of more "risk-free" interest-earning debt assets would *cause* the Collapse we are trying to prevent.

Adair Turner addresses some of these ongoing issues in the overall financial system -- and presents some longer-term solutions -- in his *Between Debt and the Devil* book.

The debt-free Money Income program offers a narrow solution to a narrower but immediate and critical problem within the commercial banking system: uncollectable creditor-assets owed as unpayable debtor-liabilities that threaten balance sheet meltdown and disorderly debt reduction by defaults and bankruptcies.

working out the details

I have outlined the debt-free money-funded Money Income program -- and its arithmetically predictable monetary and financial effects -- in broad strokes.

It really is as simple as it looks.

It would be immediately effective at "fixing" the banks' credit-debt system and solving the present financial crisis.

The IRS and Social Security Administration already have most of the citizen ID, contact information and bank account information that would be needed to implement the direct deposit payments of the Money Income program. Banks have all the customer loan account information to apply the Money Income deposits to paying down debtors' debts.

But there are many details I have not addressed, which will need to be addressed by any monetary and fiscal administrators and bankers who are involved in implementing this kind of program.

For example, millions of Americans do not have bank accounts. Some people propose creating postal banks, which are common in other countries. The US Postal Service -- which already has 10s of thousands of branches located all over the country, including many small places where there are no banks -- could be incorporated into the program.

People who are presently unbanked could have postal bank accounts to receive their Money Income deposits, and to gain access to the electronic payments system; rather than cashing their checks at payday lenders and doing all their financial business -- utility payments, etc -- standing in lines each month waiting to pay their bills in cash.

Milton Friedman once quipped that the central bank could be replaced by a laptop computer that automatically increases the money supply by 2% per year.

A "payments bank" is an electronic accounting system that debits payer accounts and credits payee accounts. You don't need buildings. You need computers. Creating postal banks involves integrating postal bank computers into the already in place central-commercial bank-operated payments system.

The postal banks could offer debit cards and online and mobile (cellphone) banking. Postal bank customers would receive their Money Incomes by direct deposit and spend their Money Incomes electronically. By arrangement with commercial banks, postal bank debit cards could be used to make cash withdrawals from commercial banks' ATMs.

Ellen Brown -- national President of the (US) Public Banking Institute -- speaks and has published extensively about this kind of "public banking".

So you can do an online search for Ellen Brown to find her books and articles; and you can visit the Public Banking Institute's website -- publicbankinginstitute.org --for more information.

Another alternative is that people could have central bank accounts.

People's Money Income could be direct deposited into their central bank accounts; and the central bank could issue debit cards, and offer online banking and cellphone banking, that enables people to spend their Money Incomes electronically within the payments system.

The central bank is already integrated into the payments system. And, again by arrangement with commercial banks, central bank account customers could use the commercial banking system's ATMs to make cash withdrawals from their central bank accounts.

Or the most obvious solution: commercial banks could open deposit accounts for the presently un-banked millions of people.

This is the simplest solution, because commercial banks already issue debit cards, operate online and cellphone banking, own the cash-dispensing ATMs, and are integrated into the electronic payments system.

Regardless what kind of bank -- postal bank, central bank, commercial bank -- people's bank accounts are in: the banks would charge service fees for administering customers' deposit accounts, and for providing customers access to the electronic payments system.

Government-owned postal banks and central banks can operate on a break-even (non-profit) basis. Privately-owned (by shareholders) commercial banks have to earn profits for the financial services they provide; so the banks can pay dividends to their shareholders.

knowing it must be done, and actually doing it

Monetary, fiscal and financial administrators have access to the specific information and are capable of working out solutions to all the details of implementing the Money Income debt paydown program. It is doable.

But so far, no nation is actually issuing any debt-free money to solve its monetary system arithmetic problems.

The essential thing right now is to recognize that debt-free money issuance itself is arithmetically necessary, so that nations actually *do it*.

Which requires clear understanding of the monetary nature of the problem. And the confidence to act contrary to the false conventional wisdom about money, banking and credit-debt, and macroeconomics.

Bernanke and Draghi did it for the monetary supply side of the balance sheet: QE for underwater debtor-banks to prevent US and eurobank liquidity failure that would have brought down the whole system. Draghi is still doing it. Carney has been doing it quietly. Japan has been doing it for decades.

Now central banks and governments have to address the monetary demand side of the balance sheet: QE for the underwater debtor-households; which addresses the banks' balance sheet insolvency problem of debtors' unpayable debts and banks' uncollectable earning assets.

different details for different countries

The purpose of a debt-free money-issuing program is orderly credit-debt reduction to prevent the "resolution by bankruptcies" part of the credit expansion-debt reduction supercycle. So different nations would distribute the new money differently.

The new spendable money begins in government deposit accounts in commercial banks, so it will be up to monetary and fiscal authorities -- and creditor commercial banks -- to decide how best to allocate the new money to the most critical needs.

A Money Income paid monthly into every citizen's bank account addresses a crisis of personal and household debt, for example, but that's not necessarily the only or most pressing crisis in every nation.

In the eurozone, national governments would sell their new zero interest perpetual bonds to eurozone commercial banks to get new euro bank deposits in the governments' bank deposit accounts; then the banks would sell the perpetual bonds to the European Central Bank (ECB), which would permanently expand its balance sheet by creating new euro reserve account balances in the bond-selling commercial banks' reserve accounts, to buy and hold the perpetual bonds.

Or national central banks could be included into the equation, by more complex accounting arrangements.

Heavily bond-indebted governments like Greece could use their new deposit account balances to directly paydown their bond debts owed mainly to German and French banks. The new money extinguishes the old debts.

This would restore solvency both to the effectively bankrupt debtor-nations who can't pay their bond debts, and the technically insolvent creditor-banks who can't collect their earning assets, but who are still holding those distressed assets on their balance sheets at full "collectable" value...

under regulatory forbearance policies that do not require banks to recognize that debtors' debts are unpayable and the banks' earning assets are uncollectable; otherwise known as "extend and pretend".

Governments of creditor eurozone nations (net exporters) like Germany might use their new deposit account balances to money-fund a Money Income paid to all German adult citizens, to compensate German workers for the wage and salary repression that held down producer costs and contributed to Germany becoming a financially efficient export powerhouse.

Germans might spend some of their Money Incomes paying for Greek vacations and buying Greek vacation properties, which helps revive the Greek tourism and real estate economy.

Like elsewhere, the most politically neutral allocation standard is "per capita" -- per adult citizen. But in the eurozone the most effective allocation standard might be "per nation".

Greece, with about 11 million people and a bond-debt crisis, "needs" the money more than does Germany with 80 million people.

But under a per capita allocation, Germany would get over 7 times more ECB-backed deposit account money than Greece.

Giving money to debtors simply extinguishes the new money and the old debt: a credit and a debit -- that is the purpose of the program.

But giving money to people who aren't indebted adds spendable/investible money that could inflate CPI prices and would inflate the prices of investment assets.

So there's a balance between price inflation and debt reduction.

As former Greek Finance Minister Yanis Varoufakis will tell you about the ongoing bailout loans "to Greece": Greece doesn't actually get the money. Greece receives and pays the money: a credit and a debit. German and French banks get the money as their overdue bond interest payments (the banks' business income), without reducing total Greek bond debt.

Under a eurozone Money Income program, Greece could actually paydown its otherwise unpayable bond debts.

Solvency would be restored to German and French banks who would get new ECB reserve assets to replace distressed debt assets (unpayable Greek bond debts) on their balance sheets; and Greece would use its Money Income to pay its way out of debt bondage.

a simple solution to a fixable problem

This debt-free Money Income program is a simple solution to a fixable problem. It enables orderly debt paydown to prevent disorderly debt reduction by mass debtor defaults, credit-debt writedowns, and catastrophic money and asset losses.

The Money Income program will not solve all of society's financial, economic and social ills. It does not even address those problems. It is a monetary solution to a monetary system problem. That's all.

Other people are working at solving all of the other problems.

Mixing complicated solutions to those other problems into this simple solution to the monetary system problem -- trying to create a "one solution for all problems" program -- will produce one guaranteed outcome:

Nothing will happen at all.

Political deadlock will be raging while bond debt-financed World War 3 is disguising the banks' balance sheet arithmetic problem by keeping the credit-debt expansion going.

Government bond debtors will pay the $trillions of new bank deposits to private sector payees (soldiers and suppliers) who can use their new deposit account incomes to paydown their old loan account debts.

And, like usual, total government bond debt will *permanently* increase, as governments pay their bond debt-financed War costs with newly created bank deposits.

I hope we can all agree that ever-increasing total credit-debt is not a "solution".

It's time to actually paydown the debts to a realistic level.

The debt-free Money Income program would enable that.

Epilogue

This *Road to Debt Bondage* book is a short version of a much more detailed book I published in 2017, *The Money Problem and How to Fix It*.

With money, complexity is the enemy of understanding.

But in the first book, I wanted to present all of the complexifying historical, technical, and monetary mechanics details, just to show that I wasn't "missing anything" in my description of the money system.

In the Money Problem book I presented many more of the historical and present macroeconomic and monetary analysts, and monetary reformers -- and their reform ideas.

Some of the recent monetary reformers -- like Britain's Positive Money group; and Jaromir Benes/Michael Kumhof's 2012 paper, *The Chicago Plan Revisited* (which revives and updates Irving Fisher's original 1930s plan from the Chicago School of Economics); recent monetary macroeconomists like Richard Koo; and Michael Hudson -- probably the foremost authority on monetary and economic history going back to the very beginning; are well worth looking into for clarity of understanding.

Most people today know the "later" version of Milton Friedman as the intellectual architect of IMF structural adjustment programs that imposed austerity so bond-indebted governments could pay their bond debts instead of paying their program spending.

But the "early" Milton Friedman -- who learned monetary macroeconomics at Irving Fisher's alma mater (the Chicago School) -- was a brilliant monetary macroeconomist who knew how the money system works and advocated financially, economically and socially beneficial ways to "fix it".

In order to be accepted into the ranks of the "authoritative consensus" that rules mainstream macroeconomics, Friedman confessed his faith in neoclassical barter economics in his 1962 book, *Capitalism and Freedom*,

"Despite the important role of enterprises and money in our actual economy, and despite the numerous and complex problems they raise, the central characteristic of the market technique of achieving co-ordination is fully displayed in the simple exchange economy that contains neither enterprises nor money." {p.14 in the University of Chicago Press 40th Anniversary Edition of *Capitalism and Freedom*}

Which means there are no money-spending consumers; and no profit-seeking businesses (enterprises) paying out their costs in money and earning sales revenues and profits in money. There are only producers trading the "exchange value" of their supplies of tradable goods with each other. Which is what is taught in the economics schools as "reality".

To his credit, Friedman never abandoned his monetary understanding in the face of the "authoritative consensus" of mainstream macroeconomics that models the workings of a hypothetical (imaginary) barter economy and insists that money -- and credit-debt creating banks -- are not "real".

It was Friedman who originated the 1969 "helicopter money" idea that Ben Bernanke made famous in a 2002 speech, for example. The central bank can end a deflationary depression by printing money and dropping it out of helicopters. People would pick up the "free money" and spend the moribund economy back to work producing stuff for sale.

I describe more of the early and late "Friedmanisms" in the first book. But I just wanted to mention the early Friedman here, to prevent readers from thinking I am a supporter of austerity programs which are the direct opposite of what the economy needs.

I will include all of the articles, papers, booklets and books that I cited in the Money Problem book, in the Bibliography of this Debt Bondage book.

This Bibliography is not an exhaustive list of all monetary macroeconomists and monetary reformers.

But if you want to do further research into monetary matters, the publications listed in the Bibliography are a good place to start.

Bibliography

Allen, Frederick Lewis; *The Lords of Creation*; (1935); the recently republished Forbidden Bookshelves edition (2014) added the sub-title, *The History of America's 1%*

Bank of England; *Money Creation in the Modern Economy* (2014)

Bank of England; *Money in the Modern Economy* (2014)

Benes, Jaromir and Kumhof, Michael; *The Chicago Plan Revisited* (2012)

Bernanke, Ben; *Deflation: Making Sure "It" Doesn't Happen Here* (Federal Reserve Board; Remarks by Governor Ben S. Bernanke Before the National Economic Club, Washington D.C. November 21, 2002)

Brown, Ellen; *The Web of Debt: The Shocking Truth About Our Money System And How We Can Break Free* (2007, 2010)

Brown, Ellen; *From Austerity to Prosperity: The Public Bank Solution* (2013)

Butler, Smedley; *War is a Racket* (1935)

Carnegie, Andrew; *Triumphant Democracy: Or, Fifty Years' March of the Republic* (1886)

Dawney, Dr. Emma; *Sovereign Money Initiative* www.vollgeld-initiative.ch/en

Deutsche Bundesbank Eurosystem; *How Money is Created* (2017)

Douglas, CH; *Money and the Price System* (text of a 1935 speech to the King and government of Norway)

Federal Reserve Bank of Chicago; *Modern Money Mechanics: A Workbook on Bank Reserves and Deposit Expansion* (1961-1994)

Ferguson, Niall; *The Ascent of Money: A Financial History of the World* (2008)

Fisher, Irving; *Booms and Depressions* (1932)

Fisher, Irving; *The Debt-Deflation Theory of Great Depressions* (1933)

Fisher, Irving; *100% Money and the Public Debt* (1936)

Friedman, Milton; *A Monetary and Fiscal Framework for Economic Stability* (1948)

Friedman, Milton; *Capitalism and Freedom* (1962)

Galbraith, James K; *The Predator State: How Conservatives Abandoned the Free Market and Why Liberals Should Too* (2008)

Galbraith, John K; *The Affluent Society* (1958)

Galbraith, John K; *Money: Whence It Came, Where It Went* (1975)

Hoenig, Thomas; *Too Big Has Failed* (2009)

Hudson, Michael; one of Hudson's recent books is *J is For Junk Economics: A Guide to Reality in an Age of Deception* (2017)

Keen, Steve; *Debunking Economics: The Naked Emperor Dethroned* (2001, 2011)

Keen, Steve; *Can we avoid another financial crisis?* (2017)

King, Mervyn; *The End of Alchemy: Money, Banking, and the Future of the Global Economy* (2016)

Korten, David; *When Corporations Rule the World* (1995)

Kucinich, Dennis and Zarlenga, Stephen (American Monetary Institute); *Bill HR 2990, The NEED Act* (2011)

Mehrling, Perry; *The Global Credit Crisis, and Policy Response* (2009)

Mill, John Stuart; *Principles of Political Economy* (1848)

Minsky, Hyman; *Can "It" Happen Again? Essays on Instability and Finance* (1982)

Minsky, Hyman; *Stabilizing An Unstable Economy* (1986)

Pettigrew, Richard Franklin; *Triumphant Plutocracy: The Story of American Public Life from 1870 to 1920* (1922)

Piketty, Thomas; *Capital in the Twenty-First Century* (2013)

Polanyi, Karl; *The Great Transformation* (1944)

Positive Money; positivemoney.org

Public Banking Institute; publicbankinginstitute.org

Ricardo, David; *Principles of Political Economy and Taxation* (1817)

Shearer, Chant, Bond; *Economics of the Canadian Financial System: Theory, Policy and Institutions*; Third Edition (1995)

Smith, Adam; *An Inquiry into the Nature and Causes of the Wealth of Nations* (1776)

Turner, Adair; *Debt, Money and Mephistopheles: How Do We Get Out Of This Mess?* (2011)

Turner, Adair; *Between Debt and the Devil: Money, Credit, and Fixing Global Finance* (2016)

Twain, Mark; and Warner, Charles Dudley, *The Gilded Age* (1873)

Varoufakis, Yanis; *Adults in the Room: My Battle with the European and American Deep Establishment* (2017)

Waldman, Steve Randy; *the negative un-natural rate of interest* (2011)

Wray, Randall; *Debt-Free Money: A Non-Sequitur in Search of a Policy*; July 1, 2014; neweconomicperspectives.org

www.ingramcontent.com/pod-product-compliance
Lightning Source LLC
Chambersburg PA
CBHW071604220526
45469CB00003B/1118